I0424916

THE

VICARS

WIFE

Chapter 1

Jayne's latest depression had taken weeks to subside, and Jonas had ignored her unspoken pleas for help.
Sitting in the bedroom alone she contemplated her life.
Forty years old and still childless and the wife of fifty year old Reverend Jonas Beech the vicar of St Matthias's and living in the small village of Aston Meade in rural Wiltshire.
Jayne dropped the bath towel she had wrapped around her and stood to her full height of five feet six inches.
She looked at herself in the wardrobe mirror; despite her willowy stature she recognised that she still had full rounded breasts and equally firm buttocks.
She was immensely proud of her natural wavy shoulder length auburn hair that she thanked god for keeping the grey at bay.
She stepped closer and stared into her dark brown eyes that every so often she saw gave a brooding haunted impression, that she recognised had been brought on by years of her debilitating bouts of depression.
She returned and lay on her back on the bed staring at the ceiling and thought of Jonas her husband of eighteen years. She frowned as she pictured him

standing in the church his six feet straight frame, with his ridiculously combed over monks pate, and recalled his younger days as a rugby player with thick wavy dark brown hair and hard muscles that like his hair had given way to the passage of time.

She smiled as she thought of his pronounced stomach that his vanity kept hidden from his parishioners by a well laced girdle.

His deep blue eyes had always been the light that attracts the night time moths, when it comes to the women who attend his services.

With the vision of her husband once more bring her depression closer, she forced herself up from the comfort of the bed and dressed quickly before making her way to the kitchen. She looked at the clock and knew that Jonas would be locked in his study.

She poured herself a black coffee and sat at the table her mind again unwillingly retreating into her memories

It had taken a number of years for Jayne to come to accept that Jonas had a weakness for a certain type of woman, which was rather the opposite of herself.

After one such incident she suspecting her husband of a liaison with a recently widowed parishioner a full bodied lady, whose sixty year old husband's sports car ran into the rear of a harrowing machine being towed by a tractor.

His bravado of deeming not to wear his seat belt meant that he failed to recover from the coma after three months in Devises hospital.

Jonas in his role as vicar visited the grieving widow several times, and in any small community gossip is rife; much to the delight of Eric Hardcastle the postman who was also the local window cleaner in his spare time, and who is notoriously nosy and the source of many of the tales of impropriety that circulated around the village.

Eric would never say outright what he had witnessed but enjoyed the round the houses route of passing along his information.

On this occasion he inferred, which always meant he could deny ever accusing anyone of doing anything untoward; that someone who the village should be able to trust, and a lady who no longer had to be concerned about her husband catching her 'at it'; was the way Eric voiced his news in the corner of the Olde Crown bar.

Jayne overheard about Eric's window cleaning observations, in the post office, and confronted her husband that same day.

Jonas of course vehemently denied the allegation, and suggested that as this wasn't the first time she had falsely accused him of having assignations with other women perhaps it was time for her to consult a psychiatrist, to combat her apparent paranoia.

Jayne felt beaten again somehow Jonas always managed to twist her accusations so that she felt guilty and wondered if indeed she was becoming paranoid.

Deep in her mind she knew that there was more to it than Jonas would ever admit and as the days passed Jayne felt her feelings of despair building slowly.

Usually her depressions seemed to appear from out of nowhere, but this one inched its way into her mind; slowly at first, not realising that it was one of those darker moments.

Jayne eventually accepted that the overheard rumour was untrue after Jonas swore on his bible that it had no foundation whatsoever.

Over the years she had tried to understand her unwarranted feelings of hopelessness, only to be thwarted each time she felt the answer to her depressions was close.

"Are you feeling alright dear?" Jonas asked for the third time that Monday morning, which only made Jayne want to scream back at him. 'That she felt absolutely fine.' When in fact she felt anything but fine; but it was her problem not his.

"Yes, nothing is the matter, why do you continue to ask?"

"Sorry I hadn't realised I had asked previously. Just concerned I suppose, only you seem somewhat tense, that's all, but if you say you're ok, then that's fine. I have to pop into Devizes; I have another meeting with the bishop."

Jayne smiled wanly, happy that she would have some time alone.

"Would you like to accompany me; you can do a little shopping perhaps?" Jonas said pushing his breakfast plate away, and getting up from the kitchen table.

"Not today dear. I have a million things to do, and Charles wants me to assist him in tuning the organ. I do believe that he thinks my ear is more acute to the subtle sounds; either that or his hearing is not as discriminating as it once was. Probably all those years he spent working in the foundry somewhere in the midlands."

Jayne forced her mouth to create a smile while she really felt like screaming.

"Anything you want me to pick up for you then?" Jonas asked slipping his overcoat on.

"Maybe something to read, you know the sort of romantic novels I like."

This time she managed a real smile.

"Of course, take care and I'll see you around four."
He pecked her on her proffered cheek and closed the back door behind him.

He walked briskly to his old Aston Martin his father had given him when he graduated from the seminary twenty years earlier.

The car still looked as if it had just rolled off the production line, but that look had only been achieved by years of loving care and attention and several thousand pounds spent on its upkeep over the years.

The car started first time, and to Jonas ear it purred like a Rolls Royce, he allowed a minute for his ear to attempt to pick up the slightest rattle of the tappets, but smiled to himself as no disturbing sound appeared.

Satisfied that his mechanical love was running fine, his mind returned to Jayne and her recurring depression.

Smiling to himself as he knew he had weathered another storm with complete ease. His bible swearing was always the one thing that clinched her belief in him.

"If only she knew." He muttered to himself recollecting the several hours he had spent consoling the sex starved chubby widow.

Tim Harding their local GP and friend had prescribed several courses of anti depressants over the years, but they all failed to have any lasting effects, and Jonas felt that this latest one was somehow going to be a far deeper one than she had experienced for several years. And while he had some idea that he might have tried to be a little more considerate, he knew that it was something Jayne was going to have to deal with.

The Monday morning traffic was lighter than he expected, and he pulled onto the small car park of St Peters the one time church of the 12th century castle that had been built for the governor and the garrison and now where he was to meet his friend and mentor Bishop Rupert Harris.

The Bishop's car was nowhere to be seen and Jonas saw by the car's clock saw that he was almost half an hour early for their meeting.

"Just enough time to pick up a book for Jayne." He said to himself easing himself off the leather seat.

The February sunlight that eked its way though the few cumulous clouds that drifted across the pale blue sky held no warmth whatsoever and Jonas buttoned his coat and collected his scarf and gloves from the rear seat.

Clipping the steering lock carefully around the steering wheel he locked the car and strode towards the high street, with its few early morning shoppers daring to brave the bracing cold morning.

Jonas dodged down a small narrow side street and out of the biting wind and halfway down he slipped into the welcoming warmth of the small bookshop.

He found several books that he felt Jayne hadn't already read but then she seemed to devour these trashy novels especially when she was in her dark moods, and they were the genre she liked to lose herself in.

He chose two, and with still a few minutes to kill he preferred the warmth of the bookshop to the bleak car park.

Jonas meandered deeper into the rear of the cluttered book shop into its extensive second hand section.

Jonas loved the art of book browsing, especially in the second hand section where books years out of print were to be found.

He speedily ran his eye along the shelf that contained books related to religion, most were books he had read as a student written by what he felt were dullards of his faith, and his eyes flashed by them the jammed between a small green leather bound volume and a rather tattered coverless thicker book, his eyes suddenly lighted on a small obviously well used thin glossy book titled Religious Desires by a Rik Kolling, an author he couldn't recall ever coming across, and although it had been years since he felt the need to bolster his own faith by reading other peoples versions; the books title seemed to draw him, and he flipped open the cover and read the frontispiece.

Matthew 22:36:-
'Teacher, which is the greatest commandment in the Law?'
He said to him; "You must love Jehovah your God with your whole heart and with your whole soul and with your whole mind.
This is the greatest and first commandment.

The second, like it; is.
"You must love your neighbour as yourself and it is upon these two commandments that the whole Law hangs."

The third reference comes from:-
John 13:24:-
I am giving you a new commandment, that you love one another; just as I have loved you, that you also love one another.

These quotes are the basis of the book of truth upon which I have researched and committed to the world of God's undying love for both men and women

Rik Kolling

Jonas mind automatically began to argue the reality of the text when he glanced at his watch, he saw that he just five minutes before the meeting with the bishop was due to commence and the Rupert was a stickler for punctuality.

He slipped the book on top of the two romantic novels, and after paying for them strode back up the narrow street back onto the now much busier High Street.

Crossing the car park he saw the Bishop's new car alongside his own older but more luxurious one.

Smiling as he compared the two vehicles and after carefully lifting several late falling leaves from the roof and bonnet; he opened his car door and placed the plastic bag containing the books on the passenger seat.

Chapter 2

Jayne certainly didn't feel like helping Charles Durning tune the church organ, even though he always seemed to make her laugh and he had a knack of making her feel like a real woman instead of a depressive wreck.

It was not the things he said but often the way he would look at her while he said them, she was also aware that Charles was something of the counties lothario.

His startling deep green eyes would look into her own brown ones as if he was looking into her mind reading the thoughts that he inspired that she fought to control. His long collar length dark hair had just begun to grey at the temples, giving him that extra look of maturity and too many middle-aged women, desirability. It also went a long way to reduce his 'toy-boy' image enough to encourage the ladies of the so called older generation to lust a little more over him.

His slim muscular body was hidden by the ill fitting suits he wore, but it was the mixture of his male aroma and the muskiness of his aftershave and matching cologne; that would make Jayne's thoughts venture too easily off the straight and narrow.

"Jayne?" she heard his deep melodious voice drift down the hall and into the kitchen.

"Jayne are you there?" he called again.

Jayne shuddered as wild thoughts flashed through her depressed mind as if looking for something positive to cling to instead of the dark pit that threatened to engulf her.

"Yes Charles I'm just coming." She smiled as the last word emitted from her lips.

"If only." She whispered to herself bracing her shoulders back before stepping out into the long dark hallway.

Charles stood with the front door ajar his body framed in almost silhouette by the light from outside, His perfectly white teeth clearly visible by the lower reflected light from the kitchen.

"Sorry I know I am a little early, but better early than late." He said holding her coat for her to slip her arms into.

"Always the gentleman Charles." Jayne said her depression easing a little as the handsome man began having its expected effect.

"Here let me take your arm, there is a patch of ice along the path." He said catching hold of Jayne's elbow.

Jayne started momentarily it was if a sharp twinge of static electricity passed between them.

Jayne felt Charles hand tighten on her arm as he guided her over the patch of frozen water, once across he kept his hand less firmly but gently, as if not wanting to release her.

It was only when they reached the narrow ladder like steps that led up to the organ balcony did he deem to release her, and allow her to lead the way up the steep wooden stairs.

She had a sudden feeling that his eyes were gazing up her knee length skirt, as he waited for her to reach the top, and though she didn't look behind, she deliberately grasped the rails and leant backwards before taking the last two steps in one allowing he skirt to ride above her knees.

Her ears picked up the faintest of gasps making her realize that Charles had been intent on seeing up her skirt.

Jayne felt her heart kick up a gear as her breasts tingled with the lewd thoughts that raced through her mind.

"Are you coming?" She called behind her.

The final word once more brought a hint of a smile across her face.

Suddenly she recognized that she was flirting with her own thoughts, and wondered what Charles would say if he could indeed read her mind.

"Indeed I am." Charles replied attempting to push the all too brief image of Jayne's white gusset that his lecherous eyes had feasted on.

Jayne sat on the right side of the double organ seat and began pumping the paddles.

Charles slid beside her until his upper thigh lay against hers.

Again Jayne felt the twinge of static electricity that flowed between them.

Seeing his dry smile caste towards her, she felt he was reading her very private thoughts and she felt a damp warmth settle beneath her bottom.

"You look a little down." Charles said "Are you sure you want to do this today?"

"Yes of course, just one of my depressions threatening to overwhelm me, but it'll pass." She said hopefully.

"Would it help to talk about it? I know its not easy to talk to someone who is too close to you, as much as they try to understand, they never really do, and it can be extremely frustrating, but having someone you have known briefly, gives you just enough confidence but without the familiarity." Charles said his eyes seeking answers in her now moistening eyes.

"You seem to know something about depression." Jayne whispered, as if not wanting to be overheard by the long dead corpses buried beneath the large heavy flagstones in the church below.

"My mother and sister were both life long sufferers, and I learnt a lot from seeing them cope with the agony of it. It was our local priest who used to spend hours just listening to them unburden all their fears and disturbing thoughts on him."

"Are you Catholic then?" Jayne asked surprised, she had naturally assumed that as he played the organ in an Anglican church, he would automatically have been of the same faith.

"Agnostic for want of a better word." He answered smiling, seductively Jane thought, as another warm flush settled between her tightly closed legs.

"What happened to your mother and sister? Jayne asked wanting to avoid a religious discussion.

"Mom died several years, after overcoming her depression, and." He laughed lightly. "Moira that's my sister, well she and the priest got married, after he left the church of course; they now have three boys and he is a Methodist minister on the outskirts of Auckland New Zealand suffice to say Moira too has overcome her depressive moments, and tells everyone that, with a husband and three boys she doesn't have time to think about herself anymore."

16

Jayne smiled genuinely this time picturing a priest being married with children.

"And I guess they are still happy."

"As Larry." Charles chuckled.

"So Jayne if you ever just want to talk, and I mean about anything; I will be there to listen, but never to judge and never to reveal anything you want to say to another soul. That in itself would defeat the whole object. Trust is what makes it work and once that trust is broken, and then it's just becomes a pointless exercise."

Jayne smiled shyly.

"But where does one start?" she asked.

"We could start with your thoughts; I mean those sometimes weird images that pass through our minds that when we try to analyze them, we begin to feel that we are perhaps going crazy."

Jayne suddenly recalled her thoughts about Charles and even as she tried desperately to control herself, she felt her face and neck flush instantly.

"Well perhaps we should start somewhere else." Charles said seeing Jayne's evident embarrassment.

"Possibly we might just talk about life, as it feels to you, anything really; it's about letting your mind relax."

"I don't know where to start?" Jayne felt suddenly very foolish, and was beginning to wish she could end the conversation.

"Look Jayne I feel you are letting this get to you, and it's rather the opposite effect we are looking for. So ok tell me how you and Jonas met."

Jayne's tension melted away and she began to talk, hesitatingly at first, but as Charles listened without comment or expression, Jayne relaxed and the words flowed.

She told Charles about how Jonas had actually run into her with his car, and called her all sorts of names believing she had damaged his beloved Aston Martin. She explained that his onslaught had brought her to a flood of tears.

She omitted telling him that she was just leaving an abortion clinic, and had been in a daze, and seeing her bus across the busy road had just dashed out.

She continued that Jonas had after seeing that his car hadn't sustained any damage had apologized profusely and driven her home.
"Jonas," she told him was in his second year at the Anglican College, and he had exchanged letters for a little over a month, then his letters stopped as his studies became more demanding.

She also felt unable to reveal that after her disastrous and at times brutal relationship with her aborted child's father that had lasted two years and broke up the day she informed him that she was pregnant.
Nor did she go into the fact that men ceased to interest her, but she was still desperate for love, and how Theresa her landlady, a woman ten years her senior had learnt that Jayne's affaire had ended disastrously, and had comforted her.
She also kept secret that she and Theresa spent two years in an exciting sexual affaire that Jayne admitted to herself was more satisfying than the heterosexual liaison she had lived through.

Jayne did explain that her landlady, who was also a close friend, had died of breast cancer at an early age, and that her death had occurred at the same time that Jonas graduated from the seminary.

"Jonas had been appointed as curate at St Bartholomew's church, just several streets away from the flat where I was living." she added,

She continued to explain that Jonas had called round to see how she was getting on, and apologized for losing touch, and that same day took her to dinner.

Jayne omitted telling Charles that she was on the rebound from her lesbian affaire, and that she never entertained any idea that she might find another female partner.

Jayne appreciated that Charles had been right about talking, even though she had left out the more personal events of her life up till then, she felt so much easier in her mind.

But she couldn't shake off the impression that Charles was able to get a lot more than she intended from her monologue, and it made her feel that he was anything but judgmental, and the warmth of his body seeped into her thigh, adding a moment of sexuality that Jayne felt was hers alone.

"Dear me look at the time, and we haven't even begun tuning the organ. Jonas will be back soon expecting his dinner. Would you like to stay and eat with us?" Jayne asked shyly feeling his eyes once more looking into her aroused mind.

The thoughts she relived behind the words she spoke, had rekindled those images from her past that she had tried so hard to bury when she became the wife of the newly appointed vicar of St Mary's.

"I wish that I could, but I have a friend who is in need of my help. Apparently her partner has abandoned her and gone and married my friend's brother."

Jayne frowned as she attempted to comprehend the schematics of the described relationship.

Charles smiled and explained.

"Yes the lady in question is what is termed gay, but a truly wonderful and loving woman, who is completely devastated by her partner's decision especially as it is with her brother."

Jayne blushed, despite trying desperately not to, and knowing that Charles eyes were boring into her.

"Some other time then." Jayne said not wanting to pull her leg away from his touch.

"That would be nice, so long as Jonas doesn't object." He replied standing up.

"Surely not, Jonas loves to have someone else to talk to over the dinner table from time to time."

"Can we actually tune the organ tomorrow morning?" Charles asked, helping Jayne to her feet, his hand sending a tingling sensation through her own fingers.

"Of course; Jonas usually locks himself in his study on Tuesdays to compose his coming Sunday's sermon; and the organ has to be perfect for the wedding on Saturday."

"Till tomorrow then, at nine, if that's ok." Charles said.

Jayne managed to mutter a whispered "Yes." as Charles climbed down the steps and waited until Jayne was safely on the cold flagstones; again managing to sneak a glimpse of her long slender legs and another brief view of her white panties.

Chapter 3

Jonas pulled the garage door closed behind him after running the chamois leather over the paintwork and patting the bonnet affectionately before hurrying across the drive and into the kitchen.

"Hello dear how did the meeting with the Bishop go?" Jayne asked.

"As usual, I think sometimes he just gets bored and wants someone to talk to." Jonas replied absentmindedly, trying to remember much about what they discussed.

"Did you manage pick me up a book?" Jayne asked hopefully.

She knew it was going to be hard trying to sleep tonight without a book to calm her nerves.

"Yes sorry I left them on the front seat; I'll fetch them after dinner.

By the way what do we have for dinner, I am starving. Cucumber sandwiches went out with the Second World War, but the Bishop still serves them to all his visitors.

"Beef bourguignon." Jayne replied seeing her husbands eyes light up.

"Splendid, just right for this sort of weather." Jonas replied.

"Did Charles manage to tune the organ?" He asked between mouthfuls of his favourite meal.

"Not quite." Jayne answered "We rather got to talking about a lady friend of his who has something of a problem and he wanted a woman's opinion." Jayne lied without blinking, and she was certain her husband wouldn't understand Charles talking therapy.

With a large double single malt in his hand Jonas lay back in the deep armchair with the haunting tones of Verdi's Jerusalem filling his head through the large expensive headphones.

Jayne sat opposite and switched off the television set that no longer had anything she considered worth watching.

Seeing Jonas absorbed in his music she slipped unnoticed out of the large comfortable lounge and into the garage, where she retrieved the plastic bag of books from the front seat.

She nodded gratefully, seeing three books instead of the single one she had requested.

It was late and rather than disturb Jonas and his Verdi she stole up the stairs and undressing clambered into bed wearing the new warm but uninspiring ankle length nightgown that Jonas had bought her for Christmas.

She switched the bedside reading light on and emptied the bag onto the duvet.

Two recognized authors fell upwards and Jayne winced with disappointment as she recalled that she had read both of the books several years earlier.

Disappointed she placed them on the bedside table and picked up the third well worn book with the unenthusiastic title Religious Desires.

She winced at the name, and the author, she had never heard of Rik Kolling and with nothing else to read she opened the cover.

The religious extracts on the frontispiece made her almost discard the book altogether, as she realized that Jonas had obviously bought the book for himself.

Frustrated by her lack of reading choice she opened the book at a random page, and began to read.

After two sentences she slammed the book shut, her breathing was coming fast and furious and her mind racing.

She nervously opened the book again and read another section.

She looked nervously round as if expecting someone to be watching her.

Closing the book again, she turned to the first page, and began reading the religious text with a new meaning.

She wondered if Jonas knew what the contents were, but from the years she had been married she guessed that he hadn't read beyond the cover and had assumed it was to do with religion, and not what the contents were really about.

With her ear tuned into the lack of sound coming from downstairs, Jayne turned to the first page, and began reading.

The story unfolded slowly at first but soon the interaction between the fictitious buxom wife of a clergyman and a female parishioner, brought a wry smile to Jayne's face.

As the accidental reaction developed between the two fictitious women soon evolved into an extremely sexual and passionate affaire that surpassed Jayne's own experiences with her landlady lover from previous years.

The things she read brought a whole new outlook to a lesbian affaire, things she wished she and Theresa had know and experienced.

Jayne's heart was racing and she hadn't realized that her hand was clamped firmly in the vee of her crutch.

Her whole body tingled with erotic passions she hadn't felt for years, and as further revelations flooded from the pages, she pulled up her nightgown up to her waist and her fingers found her swollen love button.

With her eyes absorbing the words from every page she slowly masturbated until she felt herself explode into her hand.

And still she wanted more, so with her fingers deep inside herself she milked herself, feeling the wet patch spreading beneath her bottom, and the musky aroma of her personal sexual activity seemed to fill the bedroom.

The sudden noise from downstairs made Jayne jump and instantly she slammed the book closed and slid it beneath her pillow.

The aroma of her sex was obvious and the sound of the light being switch off downstairs sounded like a bullet shot in the quiet bedroom.

Jayne leapt out of the bed and grabbed the body deodorant and hastily sprayed it around the room.

She barely made it back into bed before the bedroom door opened and Jonas strode in sniffing the air.

"Bit potent dear in here." he said sneezing as the atomized perfume irritated his nostrils.

"Just freshening the bedroom, I forgot to open the window this morning." Jayne lied burying her head under the duvet.

Chapter 4

"Hello Charles you're later than I expected, did the tuning job take longer than you anticipated."

The thirty-six year old slim but well proportioned Sally Monroe said sitting in the middle of her soft three seater deep sofa, her eyes still red from crying.

"Would you believe that Yvonne that heartless bitch wants me to pack up the rest of her stuff? And get this; she wants to know if you would take it round to the bastard brother of mine's flat."

"I suppose I could do that." Charles said his eyes seeking out the distraught Sally's hazel eyes.

"Charles when you look at me like that my legs go weak and I forget that my prelediction is for my own sex." She said smiling for the first time in days.

"Best to try all the food on the table before deciding what dish tastes best, also eating the same food can sometimes get a little monotonous. I mean you don't have to fall in love with one dish you can also appreciate other flavours."

"Maybe you are right, and just maybe it's what I need to get my revenge. I just know she would hate to think of me being deliciously reamed by a good looking hunk like you, in fact especially you. I still remember her face when you refused to fuck her years ago." She looked seductively at him.

"That was different, she had just taken up with you, and Sally you have been my friend for a long time."

"Yes I know and don't get to thinking that I haven't in the past wanted to make love to you myself. But something always seemed to get in the way, either I was involved, or you were, but now I gather we are both free of commitment. Unless of course you are setting your cap at the vicar's wife; I know she is rather dishy for her age, but I mean; a vicar's wife. Would the missionary position every night suit your needs?"

Charles laughed.

"Sally Monroe you have wonderful one track mind."

"Two tracks actually if you count both species." Sally countered.

"Touché." Charles replied wondering how long it would take Jayne to enter into an affaire with him.

"No, well not at this moment in time, I am not attached to anyone." He added knowing exactly how she would react.

Rebounders were always the easiest of seductions. Not that it was the seduction process he desired so much, but rather the boost it gave him knowing that the women he philandered with always felt happier and more confident, especially as he always insisted that there could never be anything more than an erotic interlude. He just wasn't built that way.

"You could at least kiss me." Sally said pouting her lips seductively towards him.

"That would give me more pleasure than you can imagine my dear; our friendship has always been missing that side of the fun zone." Charles said kneeling before her and holding her face between his hands and pulling her still pouting lips towards him.

His open mouth encapsulated Sally's full red lips, while his tongue teased its way between them.

Sally's mouth open wide enough for Charles tongue to enter her mouth, and her attempts to avoid his searching tongue were useless. She abandoned the task allowing his snakelike tongue to titillate her erogenous zones inside her small mouth.

In desperation she managed to catch it with her teeth, and Charles now with his tongue immobilized allowed his hand to slide up her above knee length skirt.

Sally squealed by the unexpected intrusion releasing Charles tongue.

"Witch." Charles laughed as Sally opened her legs and shuffled her bottom towards the edge of the sofa.

Her tight panties covered her damp vagina, and it was with difficulty that Charles was able to hook his fore finger in through the side of her gusset and tugging hard managed to ease it to one side.

Her long labia lips were folded up inside the vagina walls and with his constricted forefinger Charles could only manage to massage the outside of her wet vagina. As Sally's fanny responded and she became wetter, and desperate for Charles to satisfy her lust, she lifted her bottom high enough to enable Charles to drag her panties further down and over her rounded buttocks.

With two hands up the outside of her thighs Charles hooked his fingers into the waistband and drew the panties down her thighs over her knees and off her feet.

Seconds later her skirt followed over her lean flat stomach with her trimmed pubic mound with its own clear knifelike slit disappearing down between her thighs.

"That looks and smells good enough to eat." Charles whispered his eyes feasting on the glistening wetness that exposed her arousal.

"Well then hungry man what are you waiting for?" Sally giggled lifting her legs higher and wrapping her arms under her knees, revealing the whole length of her full lipped vagina with her tiny tight puckered arsehole less than an inch from the end of her wet cunt.

"Oh Charles please suck me, push your tongue up inside me. Peel it open wider and suck my clit. I want to come, in fact I fucking well need to come. Then please push you prick right up inside me and empty yourself. Or do anything else you want I just want to be used by you now." she begged desperately.

Charles allowed his mouth to cover her now sexually pungent vagina while his mouth sucked at her wetness, his tongue reamed the walls and secret folds inside her hole.

After her first orgasm Sally relaxed momentarily, and Charles tongue locked onto the shroud that kept her already emerging white tipped clitoris safe.

As the tip of his tongue peeled the many folds of her cloak backwards her erotic bean appeared more and more until it was large enough for Charles lips to pull it as far out as it was able.

His suckling motion began to make Sally shudder and pant heavily as another impending orgasm built until she could contain no longer and she screamed and clamped her legs tightly against the sides of his head, jerking spasmodically as surge after surge drained both her body and mind.

"Enough Charles please?" She begged as his lips returned to sucking her retreating clitoris to avoid the further highly sensitive sensation of Charles mouth.

Charles climbed to his knees a wet patch visibly round his own crotch, while Sally lay back with her legs tightly together.

"Still want me to fuck you?" Charles grinned "Or have you had enough?"

"For the moment, but oh yes I want to feel you filling my hole, but you don't have to be anywhere do you?"

"No I am all yours until tomorrow morning, but can I at least finish removing your clothes?" he asked sensuously.

"Do it slowly then but no touching my fanny or my nipples for a while I am tingling like I haven't felt for a long time. Even Yvonne had lost her touch over the past year, but I suppose that's because my fucking brother Reg was giving it too her." She cursed.

Charles pulled the five foot five Sally to her feet her armed locked around his neck and pulled his mouth onto hers their tongues teased the insides of each others mouth in a truly sensual moment as their bodies slowly relaxed.

Charles hardly felt Sally's hands unbuttoning his shirt or unbuckling his belt; while his own hands completed her blouse buttons and unclipped the front catch of her brassiere allowing her soft upturned size thirty-six size breasts to become free from restraint.

He gazed at the deep brown areolas with even darker dimpled nipples that stood prominently waiting to be suckled.

With her arms momentarily free Charles swept both brassiere and blouse down her arms and dropped onto them onto the sofa.

Naked she smiled and shook her deep brown hair while unzipping his trouser zip and with her small long fingered hands. She peeled both his trousers and gaudy boxer shorts down far enough for gravity to take hold.

His shirt, like her own blouse she pulled over his broad muscled shoulders, and he slipped his hands free from the unbuttoned cuffs.

Sally flung the shirt over behind her shoulder to join her own discarded clothes onto the sofa.

Only then did she allow her eyes to drop down onto his large erect blue tipped penis that had a bead of pre-come sitting in the small fishlike mouth.

Unable to resist she used her forefinger to lift the tiny bead of pure nectar on it and looking him directly in the eyes she placed it on her extended tongue.

"Delicious." she said smirking like a naughty child before reaching down and wrapping her long fingers round his pulsing prick.

Slipping to her knees she pushed her tightly pursed lips over the blue edged knob allowing the edge of her teeth to drag over his tender rim making him stand on tip toe as his nerve endings screamed.

"Sally." Charles called as he fought to drag his sensitive knob from her mouth.

"Well let me bend over Charles." She begged "You can get it all the way inside me then, and please don't come too fast I want to get the full experience."

"Over the arm of the sofa then." Charles said placing one of the scatter cushions on the arm to get a little extra height.

With his hands on each side of her well rounded buttocks he pulled them apart revealing her round puckered arsehole and the pale pink insides of her heavily lipped cunt.

Slowly he let his swollen knob rest against the eager lips, pressing for several seconds before gently letting it enter slowly into her body.

He felt her muscles tighten as his large knob forced its path past the walls of her vagina that tightly gripped his thick blue veined shaft.

"Higher." Sally gasped, her fingers twisting her own nipples savagely hard sending waves of pain through her stimulated body.

As Charles balls slapped against her pubic bone. Sally bore down one set of fingers still ravaged her nipples while the others set began to tug almost unmercifully on her extended inch long clitoris.

"Fuck me hard Charles. Please do it now let me feel your spunk flood my cunt." Sally begged urgently wanting to feel Charles cock thrusting up inside her.

Charles began slowly speeding up as Sally screamed for more.

Sally exploded three times before Charles allowed his own balls to send its seed roaring deep inside Sally's pounded vagina.

Sucking in desperately needed oxygen they collapsed onto the discarded clothes on the settee.

"Charles that was fucking wonderful it made Yvonne's efforts so bloody insignificant." she said allowing him to watch his semen dribbling down the inside of her legs.

"That looks nice." He cackled.

"Bloody cold when it gets to my knees." she replied wiping her hands up her legs, and licking his semen off her fingers.

Chapter 5

Jonas was up early the next morning and took his coffee and toast into his study and locked the door to ensure that he could write his sermon and deal with the other paperwork that his position demanded; and he needed privacy and time to examine the latest photographs that went with consider the Bishops proposal.

The sound of the bedroom door closing woke Jayne from the erotic dream that seemed to have gone on all night.

As she opened her eyes she knew that her body was in a state of total arousal, her breasts tingled and her vagina throbbed with a physical need she had thought was only obtainable when one was younger.

She slipped her hand between her legs in an attempt to smother the desire only to discover that as her fingers brushed her aroused sex button it became to much to bear and unable to resist she spread her legs wide open beneath the duvet and caressed he clit until she couldn't hold back and smothering her scream of her orgasm with her pillow as she allowed it to undulate through her entire frame.

Lying quietly she listened to the house noises, and waited until she heard the study door close and the distinctive click of the heavy lock's key being turned.

Slipping silently out from under the duvet she dragged the sheet from off the mattress and pushed it into the laundry basket.

The pillow cases followed finally the duvet cover itself topped up the wicker basket.

She retrieved fresh bedding from the long wooden ottoman at the foot of the bed and struggled to turn the mattress so that the damp patch from where her bottom had lain during the night was now underneath.

Jayne remade the bed and quickly dressed in a short sleeved vee neck blouse.

The thin lace bra she had carefully chosen to wear was virtually transparent revealing a faint but almost invisible image through the brassier and the blouse.

The flared flowered skirt was more of a summer one, but Jayne felt it allowed her legs to breathe.

The matching lace panties were certainly not her usual underclothes but after her nights dreams she wanted to encompass the feeling of sensuality, and she knew that sitting beside Charles would excite her, but she was determined not to allow herself to blush.

She downed the glass of iced water and slipping into a long knee length cardigan, she tripped across to the church.

The clock said eight twenty, which meant that she had a forty minute wait before Charles appeared.

Jayne smiled as her thoughts outpaced the reality of the life she had become used to.

She climbed the ten wooden steep steps to the organ balcony and sat deep in her erotic thoughts.

A small noise suddenly echoed around the empty building, making Jayne jump.

It was too early for Charles for whom punctuality was his own particular obsessive compulsive disorder.

She peeked carefully over the balustrade, and saw that it was Mary, from Grange House who after the death of her husband Teddy had volunteered to attend to the flowers arrangements throughout the church.

Jayne had forgotten that Mary usually came in on Tuesdays to remove the old flowers and prepare the vases for replenishment on Friday afternoon ready for any Saturday event, and this week there was a large wedding party arranged.

As Jayne stood up Mary glanced nervously up at the balcony.

"Jayne you almost scared me out of my knickers." She laughed. "You are really an early bird, is there something happening that I need to know about?"

"No just Charles the organ tuner is due at nine and I thought I had better be on time." Jayne said descending the steps.

"Yes indeed, dear Charles is a charming man but he is a stickler for time keeping." Mary said. "But does he really need any help. I mean he does my Grande once a year, on his own, why I don't know since Teddy passed no one ever uses it, but I know Teddy would turn in his grave if he thought I was neglecting his pride and joy."

"Yes men can be little boys when it comes to their toys, with Jonas it's his old car." Jayne smiled.

"How long has it been since Teddy died?" Jayne asked.

"Two years next week, but I have come to accept it and although I will never forget him, I have certainly moved on as teddy would have wished, and the widows and orphans group has made such a wonderful difference to my life."

"Of course your recently formed group, I never really understood all of the title. The widows is obvious but Orphans has me somewhat confused."

Mary chuckled. "Yes indeed we did wonder if you were eligible as an orphan, but being married to the pillar of our little society, we rather baulked a little, although we did agree that you were indeed an orphan."

The puzzled look on Jayne's face made her smile widen. Our orphans are those women who are abandoned in the name of work or golf, and even bimbo secretaries who we refer to as arm candy, however in your case its god himself."

"I don't understand why being married to the vicar should exclude me." Jayne said disconcertedly.

Mary blushed, "Perhaps I shouldn't have said anything and it would be indiscreet to go into detail as well as embarrassing. You must understand Jayne that we widows, and the orphans in our group are not sprightly youngsters any more, and while the bodies get older the mind seems to have got stuck and wants to share the joys of life with each other."

"Mary you make it sound wonderful, but I mean Janice, Doctor Harding's wife is a member, as is…" Jayne named several of the villages prominent residents, and for seemingly religious reasons I am to be excluded, you are not running a witches coven by any chance are you?" Jayne smiled at the thought.

"No certainly not, but then there are one or two amongst us that might be eligible. No I am sorry Jayne it's really nothing to do with any of those things. Perhaps I shouldn't have mentioned it at all but now that I have perhaps I should explain in detail. But you would have to give me your solemn oath that it would have to between just you and me, as for me it might be terribly embarrassing."

"Jayne." Charles voice interrupted Mary and Jayne's discussion.

"Pop over to the Grange when Charles has finished." Mary said making a rapid exit.

"Right Jayne shall we continue with the organ." Charles said his eyes picking out Jayne's cold swollen nipples.

Jayne caught his look and embarrassed she pulled her cardigan across her exposed chest, but deliberately forced herself not to blush, but she knew her nipples had grown even larger by Charles glance.

"A little chilly in here this morning." He said smiling allowing Jayne to climb the steps first.

Jayne held onto the hand rails letting her body lean back enough for her flared skit to hang away from her legs.

By the fourth step Charles was able to view Jayne's lacy panties the lower half of her bottom's cheeks clearly visible.

Again at the top Jayne took the last two steps in one, revealing her lacy covered crotch with its wisps of pubic hair clearly visible to the hungry eyes below.

Charles adjusted his erection so it lay flat up against his stomach before he climbed up after her.

"Considering its chilly you look rather warm." Jayne said smiling seductively.

She really intended to flirt just a little; she knew it would help move her earlier depression back from where it came.

Charles had already worked out Jayne's intention and he intended to take her to the wire. The temptation not to, was too great for him to resist.

"Do you feel we need to continue with our conversation?" Charles asked.

"Let's get the organ tuned first, and then see what time you have left." Jayne suggested allowing her cardigan to open wider revealing a fuller view of her breasts.

Jayne had noticed the upward bulge in Charles tight light tan trousers, the obvious damp spot where his penis had leaked made her own panties dampen.

The indistinct fragrance of her sexuality had begun to overwhelm the perfumed aerosol Jayne had sprayed liberally across her lower belly and between her legs.

Tuning the organ took a lot longer than either of them imagined.

Charles had to dismantle a section and replace two reeds and then to rebuild.

He kept glancing at his watch and Jayne saw beads of perspiration showed on his forehead.

The difficult cover that had taken twenty minutes to remove dropped back into place with a single push.

Charles grinned broadly.

"Thank god for that." He said quietly screwing the brass fittings home.

He played several choruses of Chopin's nocturne before declaring his work done.

Jayne leant back from her bent position and pushed her arms above her head to straighten her back, but pushing her breasts forward.

"Beautiful." Charles said unwittingly voicing his thoughts. With his eyes glued on Jayne pushed out breasts.

"What the organ or the music?" Jayne asked mischievously, her eyes fixing on Charles's groin.

Caught off guard Charles stuttered momentarily, before he regained his poise.

"Neither Jayne, truth is I was actually thinking out loud, and it was your magnificent breasts that I had involuntarily voice my opinion and I can only apologize if I have embarrassed you, but after we talked yesterday I feel it would destroy any confidence we have in each other if I were to lie to you."

It was Jayne's turn to blush, and she pulled her cardigan across her deflated nipples.

"Covering them will not make them any less wonderful." Charles said smiling. "And while I am being honest I did look up your skirt earlier when you climbed the steps. And I believe you knew that."

Jayne grinned. "Yes Charles I did know and we both know I allowed you to look deliberately. Am I shameless?"

"Indeed you are not. You are beautiful, and I also know you observed what your indiscretion did to me." He said looking down at the small dark patch at the top of his zipper.

Charles once more quickly glanced at his watch.

"I am frightfully sorry Jayne, but I have another appointment and punctuality is something I cannot avoid, but you have my number please ring me whenever you want to talk."

"Of course, but I know this is beyond anything I should ask or do as the wife of the vicar, but would you touch me, just briefly." Jayne asked brazenly.

Even before she finished speaking she felt one hand sliding up the inside of her leg and its finger hooking in the side of her panties easing it aside so it could locate her already exposed clitoris.

His other hand rose up inside her blouse and under the cup of her brassieres lifting both cups up over her breasts letting them bounce just once before his hand cupped one of them his thumb brushing across the aroused nipple.

The sound of a door closing down in the church had them apart in a millisecond.

Jayne quickly settled her breasts back into their support and they made their way back down the steps.

"Jayne, Charles, I heard the overture, and once more Charles you have the organ running superbly. I assume by the music you played that you found the box with the replacement reeds. And Jayne, I am sorry but I have to go out again; the Bishop is being a little picky; I might not be back in time for dinner so if you want to eat without me then I shall have a cold buffet when I return. I shall see you later Charles. Bye darling." He called hurrying out of the church.

"I really must go to." Charles said lifting Jayne face up by her chin and kissing her quickly on the lips.

Jayne's body took almost fifteen minutes to get back to normal, and for her breathing to calm enough for even her mind to think.

"Mary?" the thought was the first to make sense; and she remembered that she had said that she would call at the Grange.

No one answered the front doorbell after several attempts, so Jayne wandered around towards the back of the large Georgian house.

She discovered Mary in the large Victorian greenhouse, built by Teddy's great grandfather to house his collection of exotic foreign plants.

Time had changed its use and Mary now cultivated a vast array of beautiful blooms.

"Mary?" Jayne called through the foliage.

"Jayne glad you could make it." Mary replied her voice not quite as welcoming as her words.

"Coffee or something stronger?" Mary asked nervously.

"I gather something stronger might be best, by your tone." Jayne said grinning nervously.

"Whisky or gin." Mary said smiling back.

"Gin for me please." Jayne said.

"I'll have a very large whisky." Mary said hauling off her gardening gloves.

"Please let's go into Teddy's old study, its quiet and we won't be disturbed; no one but I go in there anymore."

"Aren't you alone then?" Jayne asked.

"Oh yes; but people just walk in all the time, and I can at least lock the study door.

With a wine glass full of neat gin in her hand Jayne sank into the soft high-backed chair, while Mary with her glass already half empty of Teddy's favourite single malt pulled up a chair in front of Jayne.

She took another deep gulp of the whisky, and placed it on the desk.

"Well Jayne here goes, but you will keep my confidence, no matter how it may shock you."

Jayne too took several mouthfuls wondering what on earth Mary was about to reveal.

"Of course, Mary but if you would rather not… "

"Hush just let me talk." Mary said "Otherwise I may loose my nerve." She slurred slightly and took anther drink.

"When Teddy died I was heartbroken, and I certainly had no intention of trying to replace him. And I have always been an extremely sexual woman, well on my own it became rather boring if you know what I mean."

Jayne nodded beginning to guess a little of what was coming but hardly believing it.

"Well it all began when Janice, came over one afternoon when I was feeling desperately low, apparently her husband Tim suggested that I might feel better if I had a woman to talk to. That's not to say that Tim wasn't a great deal of comfort, but he did feel that perhaps woman to woman might be more helpful.

Well of course Janice turned up, dressed to kill as usual and we talked about life in general and how she too felt the need for more from life, and so one thing led to another. We were sitting pretty much the way we are now, when out of nowhere Janice leant forward kissed me. I mean really kissed me not just a friendly kiss but a real deep sensual kiss, and she held me close to her with my head on her breasts, and the next thing I knew she had opened her blouse and I was sucking her nipple while she had her hands inside my shirt. I tell you Jayne I suddenly felt that the world had turned upside down but wonderfully so and I couldn't resist.

Jayne leant forward and caught hold of Mary's hands. And looked into the older woman's eyes that reminded her so much of Theresa's.

"Mary I understand perfectly, and did Janice kiss you like this?" Jayne whispered and pulled her mouth over Mary's letting her tongue slip between the older women's lips to find an equally busy tongue waiting for it.

As they kissed Jayne felt Mary's fingers fumbling with her blouse buttons, and her then her brassier being hoisted up over her breasts.

Jayne's hand lifted Mary's jumper over her own breasts and the pulled back from one another, Jayne

41

marveled at the large soft mounds with huge hard nipples.

Standing up Mary pulled Jayne towards her and the resumed kissing each other.

Jayne felt Mary's hands behind her waist which was followed by her skirt sliding to the floor.

Mary's hands ran over Jayne's buttocks, hooking her fingers into the waistband of her lace panties.

Slowly Jayne felt them drawn over her bottom and down to her knees where they dropped to her ankles of their own accord.

Mary unfastened her own skirt and steps out of them revealing that she was not wearing any knickers. Jayne is enthralled by the mass of pubic hair and drops to her knees and buries her face into the wonderful bush Mary's aroused vagina fills her nostrils while Jayne's tongue parts the hair her tongue eagerly searching for the swollen clitoris. With Mary's hands pressing against the back of her head, she begins moaning as Jayne's nimble tongue peels back the folds of flesh from Mary's emerging white tipped love bean,

"Suck it please?" Jayne heard Mary's franticly whispered voice.

"Jayne suck it hard. Oh my god that is wonderful more, more Mary begged her legs trembling.

"Sit in the chair." Jayne ordered helping Mary to sit in the edge of the chair.

"Jayne lifted Mary's legs over her shoulders opening her vagina wide enough for Jayne to admire the heavy dark tanned outer labia with Mary's wet pubic hair clinging to them Jayne peeled them open to see the red inner lips and the pink inner folds of Mary's open cunt.

"Suck me again Mary pleaded Make me come.

Mary's fingers pulled on Jayne's hard nipples as Jayne's head dipped back between her legs.

The insistent ringing of the doorbell resounded round the study and Jayne leapt from between Mary's legs and grabbed her clothes.

"Who is it?" Jayne gasped pulling her skirt and blouse on and pushing her underclothes under the cushion on the chair.

"Janice probably but she usually just walks in so I don't really know."

Mary was giggling as she hauled up her skirt and dragged her sweater over her head.

"Right are you decent, but perhaps you had better have another drink I imagine your breath smells a little of my fanny." Mary giggled even louder as the doorbell resonated almost angrily.

Jayne drank the remainder of the glass and spluttered as the neat alcohol hit her stomach.

Mary tidied her hair and unlocked the study door in time to see the letter box open and Janice's voice asking if she was alright.

"Just coming." Mary called back. "Well I was before you rang the bell" she muttered to herself.

She unlocked the front door.

"Hello Janice I wasn't expecting to see you today, I thought you were busy.

"I was but now I'm not, and why did you lock the front door, you never do?"

Mary smiled, Sorry but I was working out in the conservatory and as I was expecting to be on my own I decided that perhaps I should lock the front door.

"Are you alone because I thought I heard voices?" Janice asked.

"Well no not exactly."

Jayne could see both Mary and Janice's through the partially open study door through the reflection in the hall mirror.

"While Mary was talking she was trying to tell Janice to be quiet with her finger across her lips.

Janice's puzzled face couldn't seem to grasp the situation.

"No dear I have Jayne the vicar's wife visiting, and we were having a drink in the study" Mary was still visually trying to stem the flood of questions that she knew Janice was dying to ask.

"The study but you never entertain in the study."

Janice said, and by the smell on your breath you have been drinking whisky at this time of the day." Even to Jayne Janice's voice held more that a note of suspicion.

"Anyway don't stand here talking come on through and we can have a coffee in the kitchen I am sure Jayne would love one.

Jayne felt it was time for her to make an entrance and she unsteadily wove her way into the entrance hall.

The two women had only ever had a passing relationship, and neither of them could recall ever having a conversation of more that a sentence or two.

"Hello Jayne and what brings you into the ladies den on iniquity." Janice smiled.

Jayne felt her face flood with embarrassment.

"Mary wanted to discuss the flower arrangements for Saturday's wedding." She lied unconvincingly.

"Yes." Mary said even less convincingly.

"And you felt you needed to get legless to discuss such an important event." Janice giggled.

"Come on let's get some strong black coffee inside you, before your rather pious husband sees you."

Janice said helping the unsteady Jayne into the large

44

kitchen and seating her in one of the high backed stools in the corner of the units.

After three mugs of black unsweetened ground coffee. Jayne was beginning to feel that the ground was indeed flat.

Mary and Janice had sat in the lower kitchen chairs, and Janice's eyes were fixated on the slightly parted legs of the vicar's wife.

Her unbelieving thoughts were apparent to Mary, who also kept her eyes on the same spot as her friends.

"Jayne what really brought you over to the Grange, and please the flower story just didn't work, and poor Mary is about the worst liar I have ever come across."

Jayne felt herself blushing again.

"Well we were talking in the church and I asked why I wasn't welcome in your club, just because I happened to be married to my ars…Husband." Jayne knew that she still had some way to go before she was sober enough to return to the vicarage. And I sort of put Mary on the spot.

But I am rather glad I did." She said looking endearingly at the older woman.

"So that's why your blouse is done up out of sync and you are missing your knickers and brassiere, where are they under the cushion in the study?"

Jayne nodded coyly.

"I didn't have time to put them on." She giggled drunkenly.

"And how long have you known about our esteemed vicars wife?" she turned to Mary accusingly.

"Just today, and I was trying to explain a little about the Widows and Orphans and well I told her what happened between us, and then she did the very same thing, and the next thing we knew was that someone was ringing the doorbell demanding entrance.

Janice suddenly burst into a giggling fit.

"You mean nothing exactly happened?"

"Well I was just about to when you appeared." Mary smiled back, while Jayne sat wavering on the chair.

Janice pulled herself out of the chair and walking the few steps to where Jayne sat perched on the edge of the high stool."

Watching the Doctor's wife's lecherous smile as she sat back on her heels with her face level with Jayne's slightly parted legs."

"So Jayne let's see what goodies you have." Janice said her hands easing Jayne's legs apart and sliding her skirt up under her thighs.

"Would you like me to lick you?" Janice asked flicking her tongue out.

"I mean lick you right inside your cunt, and suck your clit. Looking how wet you already are I expect you would love me to make you come in my mouth wouldn't you?"

Jayne's mouth was dry she couldn't speak, but her eyes and expression was all that Janice needed and she slowly at first began to tease Jayne's open vagina apart lapping her wetness and probing as far as her tongue would let her. She watched as Jayne's already swollen clitoris emerged unaided from its hiding place.

Jayne bottom slid further over the edge of the stool and her legs were raised over Janice's shoulders.

Mary her tits are in need of your expert hands. Janice called over her shoulders.

With her blouse undone again and Mary's fingers teasing her nipples and Janice's mouth working its own miracle between her open legs Jayne felt her orgasm building slowly, until unable to contain it any further she let her body go.

46

Neither Janice nor Mary would cease their attention until Jayne resorted to begging them both to stop.

Exhausted but sober Jayne sank back in the stool and watched as Mary performed a cunnilingus ritual between Janice's spread legs, Janice all too soon reached her climax.

Now Mary you too are entitled to be love by two women so darling I suggest you put your bottom on the table, and relax.

Mary giggled but did what Janice suggested, or rather ordered.

Nervously Jayne stood beside her and held onto Mary while Janice retrieved a fresh cucumber from the refrigerator and using her versatile tongue and the long thick vegetable inserted into Mary's willing vagina.

Kiss me Jayne like you did in the study that was wonderful.

Jayne quickly clasped her mouth onto Mary's as Janice brought the open legged Mary to a shuddering orgasm.

With her underclothes retrieved from the study and her blouse buttoned correctly; the three satisfied women made their way into the more comfortable lounge with the coffee pot refilled.

"So am I a member of the Widows and Orphans now." Jayne asked felling her body respond just to the thoughts of what it all meant.

"Well I guess so but I'm not exactly sure how some of the others might respond, after all you are the vicar's wife."

"You mean they might object?" Jayne queried disbelievingly.

"Probably not I mean none of then would want their own secrets hung out with the washing, and all of them know to be careful when Eric's around."

"Eric? Oh you mean the window cleaner come postman?" Jayne laughed. "Yes Eric doesn't miss" much does he?" She added wondering about the plump widow.

"Are all the members involved in…Well you know what I mean?" Jayne asked hardly daring to believe that some of the names she knew were members could ever do the things that the three of them had done this afternoon.

"I varying degrees but none are as horny as the doctor's wife." Mary laughed.

"Not anything of a stick in the mud yourself Mary darling; I bet you could do it all again right now if we offered." Janice said winking at Jayne who smiled hopefully, as she knew Jonas wouldn't be home for at least another two hours.

"Don't you have to get back to do your husbands dinner?" Mary asked.

"Not today he's in conference with the bishop, again." Jayne said emphasizing the last word.

"Bully for the bishop." Janice laughed.

"So tell us about your secret life?" Janice added.

"What secret life?" Jayne asked feeling her colour rise.

"The one you don't think any else knows about, because that was not the first time you have had sex with a woman; now is it?" Janice said knowingly "Come on we are all big girls."

"Some bigger than others." Mary added grinning.

"Was it as good before as it was in the kitchen?" Janice pushed.

"Well I suppose it was more loving before." Jayne admitted recalling the long evenings when they would curl up naked and watch television or just talk about life, and make long seductive love until the early hours.

"It was different Theresa that was my friend was ten years older than I was and she was just so tender and loving, and I suppose not as exciting as you two, but back then I truly was in love with Theresa." Jayne felt tears of memory roll down her cheeks.

Mary put her arm round her shoulder.

"So why did it it finish?" Janice asked.

"Theresa died of breast cancer but I stayed with her right to the end, and then I had no one in my life, and that was when o met Jonas again and well he felt safe and that's about it I have been with him for almost twenty years."

"But you don't love him surely in fact I bet you never were ever in love with him." Janice asked.

"I suppose not but we get on and I suppose that's something?"

"You still think of your friend don't you? But why all of a sudden have you suddenly decided that you want to make love with women again." Mary asked.

"Of course Theresa will always be with me, but I had long given up any idea of entering into another female relationship, that was until I read a book that Jonas inadvertently bought in Devises."

"What sort of book would Jonas buy I mean as far as everyone is aware the man is a religious nut?" Janice grinned at Jayne's astonished face.

"Well I asked him to pick up a novel for me yesterday and give him his die he brought back three books two for me which I had already read years ago and one that he obviously assumed was to do with religion"

Naturally." Janice said.

"Well I only discovered that the books for me as I said I had already had them before so I decided to read his religious book. Well when I red just s few lines I realized that it was a pornographic book about a vicars wife, and when I say pornographic I mean in every detail. Suffice to say it got me all worked up so I read more, and it brought back so many happy memories. I just needed someone to love me, and well I sort of made a pass at Charles, and he well touched me, and then Mary told me about your widows and orphans and when she described how you kissed her, well I sort of lost control."

Never mind that two faced lothario, what about this book, what was it called and who wrote it?"

"Religious Delights and someone called Rik Kolling's the author

"Janice laughed no wonder your husband picked it up I would have loved to se his face when he reads it."

"Oh I couldn't let him ever read it." Jayne said horrified.

"Well can I borrow it after you have read it?" Mary interjected before Janice could ask.

"Of course but have you ever heard of the author." Jayne asked.

"I think I did several years ago there were about six books published in Bangkok caused an initial stir then no more appeared author probably died or ended up in one of their prisons, although I didn't know that his books had made their way over here. I somehow assumed that he was Scandinavian or something.

So apart from reading pornographic books Mrs. vicars wife you are certainly not as innocent as the rest of the village thinks, and I am so very pleased about that. Jayne you are a beautiful woman with a body that

50

many models would kill for, and you enjoy having sex with us, what more could a person wish for. And now even though you don't have a man to cook for I have a microwave to load up with Tim's dinner. Perhaps we could lunch over here tomorrow if that's ok with you Mary?" Janice said grabbing her Gucci handbag and kissing Jayne fully on the mouth before doing the same to Mary who slipped her hand up her departing friend's skirt.

"Don't you ever wear and knickers anymore?" She called to the departing Janice.

"Saving on the laundry bill." Janice called back.

"Would you like to stay for tea?" Mary asked.

"I would, but I shouldn't I know Jonas said he might be late, but you can never tell, and if he thinks I am off gallivanting as he calls it, he will probably sulk all evening, mind you I might go to bed early and read some more of the book.

"Well my dear if it has sort of affect on a vicar's wife all I can say is what will it do for the rest of us."

"As if you or Janice need anything if this afternoon's performance is anything to go by." Jayne suddenly felt completely at ease with both Janice and Mary, and indeed the rest of the world; much how she used to feel when Theresa was alive

Chapter 6

Jayne didn't feel much like cooking for herself, so she made a chicken salad, which Jonas could have as well when he arrived home.

After she had eaten she felt uneasy and a little on edge after all the excitement of the day, so she went upstairs and lay on the bed.

Retrieved the Religious Desires book from beneath the pillow, and making a mental promise to hide it under the mattress.

The thought of Jonas finding it, and knowing that she had been reading it, was just to frightening to comprehend.

After just one page her hormones were once more raging and she ached with desire to feel Mary's arms around her arousing her all over again.

Jayne's thoughts turned to the two older women who had sexually aroused her, she knew that Mary and Theresa looked nothing alike; but Jayne felt a kinship with Mary that reminded her of Theresa and one of the two women the author had written into his story; while Janice felt like the main character in the novel. In which so far it seemed that everything erotic was available with no restrictions that Jayne could imagine; and it made everything he had written so real and exciting.

Even as her eyes read the words that created a beautiful erotic image Jayne's fingers again sought out her aroused clitoris, and she teased it much in the manner that Mary had.

Slowly and gently in her arousing and tremendously seductive way, that allowed Jayne to extend her climax for so much longer until it allowed it like a slow moving stream rather than a huge waterfall.

It wasn't that she preferred her orgasm one way to another, but it made the whole experience much more rewarding.

"Jayne are you up there?" Jonas's booming voice echoed up the stairs.

Jayne hurriedly closed the book and pushed it under the mattress and pulled the duet over it.

"Yes dear just resting, I'll be down in a jiffy." She called back pulling the crotch of her knickers back into place.

"There's chicken salad in the fridge or I can make you something else if you like?" She said entering the kitchen.

"Salads fine." He replied a rather strange look across his face,

Jayne took the plate from the fridge and switched the kettle on.

"Coffee?" she asked "Or would you prefer a whisky?"

"I think we should both have a whisky." He said thoughtfully avoiding her eyes.

Jayne poured him a large one while she had one half its size; a fact that did not go unnoticed by her husband.

Jonas picked at his meal before pushing it away half eaten.

"Sorry I am not really very hungry." He said as if puzzling what to say next, which was not at all like Jonas.

"Did you manage to sort things out with the bishop, only you don't seem quite yourself this evening?" Jane asked hoping that the events of her unusual day had not somehow come to his attention.

"Yes and no, well I suppose I should come straight out with it." He said regaining something of his usual composure.

"With what? Has something terrible happened?" Jayne asked.

"No, no nothing at all like that, it's just that the bishop has been planning a six week traveling symposium across the north of England; and he has asked; well it's a little stronger than asked. He had informed me that I am indispensable and therefore I have to go with him.

I know that I should have discussed it with you, but I wasn't at all sure that he expected me to go with him, and up until this morning it was all up in the air; and the crux of the matter is we have to leave first thing in the morning; so it's all really something of a rush." He said thankful he had managed to tell her everything without her interrupting.

"What about the church and the wedding planned for Saturday?" Jayne asked afraid to show how relieved she was to hear that he would be away for six long glorious weeks; especially now that she had Mary and Janice to fill the empty void in her life, and of course there was also Charles, who she knew would love to get into her knickers.

This was a freedom she couldn't have ever dared hope for.

"Oh regarding the parish and the church services, the bishop has arranged for a recently graduated older student to take over my duties for the six weeks; and of course there is the spare bedroom. Apparently he is a sociable sort who came to religion later than most young men and I have been assured that he is adept at looking after himself, so he should be little or no hindrance to your own routine.

I can't recall his name, but he is supposed to arrive sometime tomorrow evening from Belfast. Apparently that's where his origins are, although I know little else about him, but I am sure he will fit in admirably."

Jayne nodded hardly daring to speak lest her joy be recognized. But the thought of another vicar about the house was somewhat frustrating.

"Well my dear I had better pack what clothes I need, and have an early night the bishop is sending his man over with the car at six o clock in the morning. So if you don't have any further questions I will say goodnight, and I will try not to wake when I leave."

As he closed the door behind him Jayne stood up and with her fixed on the closed door she punched that air and screamed a silent hurrah.

She lay awake after sleeping for a couple of hours at first listening to Jonas snoring and finally she heard him padding silently round the room while she feigned sleep.

She heard the bedroom door open and listened as he crept down the stairs.

Opening her eyes and spreading herself across the whole bed she lay there watching the clock as it, all too slowly crept to the magical hour of six o clock.

It was just five to six when she heard the limousine pull up on the gravel driveway, and she waited for the almost indiscernible clunk as the car boot and the doors closed.

She crept to the window and peeked out from behind the closed curtains and watched as Jonas was driven off on his symposium.

She returned to the bed and again spread-eagled herself on top of the covers and waited a good fifteen minutes, in the event Jonas may have forgotten something and returned.

At exactly a quarter past the hour she knew she was completely alone in the vicarage, and she peeled off her long unfashionable nightgown and threw it across over the chair and danced round the bedroom naked.

"Fucking good riddance you lousy bastard." she said in a whisper at first, and then when nobody answered; she said it louder, adding every swearword she had ever heard.

For six long glorious weeks she was going to be practically free to do what she wanted; where and how she wanted; except of course for the deputy vicar, who would probably be some wimpy guy who felt that as he approached his mid life crisis he discovered a god that had saved him.

Well she no intention of allowing this second sanctimonious prick to impinge of her new lifestyle even if it was just for six weeks.

He had Jonas's study in which to work and the spare bedroom in which to sleep, beyond that he could cook his own meals, and she had no desire to be his skivvy.

She promised herself that she would be courteous and polite and that was all.

She climbed into the shower and turned the water to as hot as she could stand, before turning it to almost cold and she relished the stinging cold water that bombarded her flesh. After taking the shower head from its stand she turned the head to the smallest and fiercest jet, and spreading her legs apart she allowed the cold jet of water to blast between her legs, finally she could take no more and she ended her ablutions, and after a quick rubdown with the towel, she made her way down stairs to the kitchen still stark naked.

A sudden thought startled her, as she tried to remember if it was Eric's day to clean the windows.

Realizing that it was the following week she spread her arms wide open at the kitchen window, just in time to see Eric walking up the drive in his postman's uniform and a bundle of letters in his hand.

His eyes seemed to be looking directly at her.

Jayne squealed and dashed for the stairs, her heart pounding as she cursed her stupidity and imagined Eric expounding his latest scandal about the vicar's wife dancing in the kitchen stark bollack naked.

"She dived beneath the duvet giggling like a school girl, at the thought of being stark bollack naked. She pushed her hand down between her legs.

"No bollacks." She whispered and held onto her sides as they ached from her laughter.

She waited until she heard Eric's van drive off before she scrambled out from under the duvet and opening the wardrobe she took out the short, above the knee length dress, which Jonas complained about her wearing commenting that it was unseemly for a vicar's wife to wear such clothes.

Jayne slipped it over her head.

"I can't be bothered to wear a bra or knickers for that matter. I don't care if it is cold I have only myself to please. So Jonas you pious prick I will wear and what I like."

After a poached egg on toast with a home made Hollandaise sauce, she spent the morning reading more of her book, often going back and re-reading several pages in case she had missed anything. She sat in the small easy chair with her feet propped up on a kitchen chair, and her hand pressed over her uncovered vagina.

As more of the story unfolded she felt her emotions flow and ebb much the same as her magic button emerged and retreated with the flow of the fictitious characters in the book.

Her mind relating to each of the females characters in turn and mental combinations of Theresa, Mary and Janice filled the other rolls.

Charles barely managed to take over the fictitious manly descriptions, but she had no one else except of course Janice's husband Tim, but somehow that just didn't seem right to imagine your new friend's husband doing those wonderful outrageous things to her. So she created her own adorable character.

It was the clock striking midday that suddenly roused her.

"Mary's." She said to the empty kitchen seeing that the morning had gone nowhere and she had promised that she would go over to the Grange for lunch.

As she made her way the short distance to Mary's mansion not giving a thought to what Mary had prepared for lunch.

Her appetite for food was not what was on her mind instead she hoped that dessert would be served between Mary's or Janice's open legs.

The book again had taken its toll in arousing her already excited hormones

She found Mary in the small paved patio adjacent to the greenhouse conservatory.

The twenty yard flagged square was surrounded on two sides by a six feet high garden wall that was covered by rows of pear trees anchored to the original Georgian bricks.

A two feet high balustrade made up the one and a half of two remaining sides.

In the centre was a five foot diameter round marble table and six caste iron garden chairs. Three of which had brightly coloured duck-down cushions tied to their hard seats.

Janice had already arrived when she heard Mary's answering call.

"We are behind the conservatory, Dear"

"Coffee?" Janice asked already pouring it from the large thermos pot into the bone china mug.

"Please, and its lovely here." Jayne said dropping her bottom onto the empty chair.

"A wonderful sun-trap cunningly built when the Grange was first constructed, so I can claim no credit for it." Mary admitted.

"So you look exceedingly happy today, I hope we can claim some of the credit for that?" Janice said smiling wantonly.

"Yes I suppose you both were, partially." Jayne replied returning a similar smile.

"Why what else has lifted your spirits?" Mary asked curiously.

"Two things really." Jayne replied knowing she was dragging out her news.

"Jayne for pity sake spit it out." Janice said seeing that their new found lover was milking the moment.

"My god you haven't been indiscreet with the organ tuner, and been tuning his organ, have you?" She added leaning forward in anticipation.

"No of course not. It's nothing like that." Jayne replied hastily, her mind picturing Charles aroused organ in her hand.

"The book. Yes that's what it is you have been reading more of that pornographic book, haven't you?" Janice squealed in delight as Jayne's face revealed that she had hit the nail on the head.

"Yes, I suppose so; it really does get the juices flowing, so to speak." Jayne relied shyly.

"So what's the first thing you did say that there were another two?" Mary asked hoping that the book Jayne was getting so excited about would soon be in bed with her.

"Jonas." Jayne said finally.

"Jonas, whatever can he have done to make you look so happy?" Janice asked looking curiously into Jayne's face.

"He's gone away on a symposium with the bishop for six whole weeks." She finally exclaimed.

"Six wonderful weeks without him. Is that awful of me to be happy about that?" she asked.

"You are talking about your husband Jonas, the vicar of the parish aren't you, and you said 'gone'?" Janice asked.

"Yes of course I don't know any other Jonas, and he left at six o clock this morning."

"Then my dear it is certainly not awful of you and you have every right to be ecstatic. I certainly know I would if I was married to him." Janice leant forward and gripped Jayne's hands.

"In six weeks your world is going to change forever; believe me it has already begun." She said pulling

Jayne towards her and kissing her tenderly on the mouth.

"So more coffee anyone?" Mary asked holding the flask up.

"Please." Jayne and Janice chorused.

They sat sipping the unsweetened brew soaking in the meager warmth of the winter sun.

"What are we to do without a vicar?" Mary asked. "I mean there's supposed to be a wedding in…" she made a quick calculation. "…in four days."

"That's the downside." Jayne replied. "The bishop has appointed a temporary vicar, a mature graduate Jonas called him, who by the way is supposed to arrive around dinner time this evening, and he comes from Belfast."

"Oh my giddy aunt, you mean we are to have geriatric bog trotter as our new vicar. Well I can see that going down well in the village." Mary said seriously.

"You never know he might not be as bad as we think." Janice said giggling.

"No he might be a bloody sight worse." Mary unfettered breasts bounced as she chuckled.

"So where is he staying surely not at the vicarage with you?" Mary asked still barely containing her amusement. "I mean what will people think; you alone in the same house as a bog trotting savage from the streets of Belfast?"

"Mary I have met a number of people from Belfast and other parts of Ireland and they are wonderful lovely people. Theresa's parents came from Belfast years ago; her mother was Catholic and her father protestant." Jayne said feeling the joke had gone a little too far.

"Yes I'm sorry, of course you are right, and here we are condemning this poor older man even before we have met him. But I still maintain that people will talk if he stays in the vicarage." Mary said apologetically.

"Well that's where Jonas has already arranged for him to stay, so if Jonas trusts me then so should the rest of the village." Jayne replied cautiously creating an image of the new vicar in her mind and shrinking away from it.

"So enough of my news please tell me more about the widows and orphans." Jayne asked wanting to think of something other than her lodger for the next six weeks.

"I'll let Janice tell you while I prepare lunch. Homemade chicken and mushroom soup with home baked bread do for you both." She asked levering herself up from the table, anyone want a shawl or something its getting a little chilly now that the sun seems to have given up for the day.

"Just the soups fine for me." Janice said her eyes fixed on Jayne's protruding nipples and brushing her hand over her own equally swollen buds.

"Same for me." Jayne called.

"Well so what exactly happens when all you widows and orphans get together?" Jayne asked.

"I suppose you imagine that we have a wild orgy with everyone naked and molesting each other?" Janice said grinning mischievously. "Well so far it's nothing like that; in fact it's all very… well sort of normal. I mean civilized, absolutely nothing like what happened yesterday. Mary and I are perhaps somewhat different from the others, not that there are a huge number, I know you have heard several names mentioned, but as you can imagine we don't tend to broadcast our membership."

Jayne nodded appreciatively certainly not wanting her own name bandied about. One wrong word in Eric's ear and who knows what the consequences could be.

"So we usually get together about every three months or so, sit around and chat, and just see what happens and invariably something does after Mary's exceedingly potent punch bowl needs refilling, and those who want privacy have several rooms they can use, but often as not we find that those that want to do what they want to, just seem to get into it, and well the rest of us tend to enjoy watching each other reach that state of climax that for all of us is so rewarding. But there is certainly no pressure on anyone.

There are still two of our latest recruits who have yet to imbibe at our meetings however in private they are beginning to enjoy a life they never dreamt existed."

"And what about you?" Jayne asked her fingers hidden beneath the table were teasing her clitoris through her thin dress.

"Me, well I suppose I have always been this way, I adore making love, having sex, call it what you will. Even when I was quite young it was the only thing that interested me, and I would masturbate almost continuously for hours.

This is why I believe my parents finally sent me away to an all girl's boarding school, where they thought I would be beyond temptation of boys, Well girls were so much better at it than the immature boys, and with the six formers being as horny as hell we learnt so much and had so much sex it was unbelievably a great experience.

But like all young girls I became infatuated with my French teacher, him being the only man in the whole school, and in great demand.

I learnt long after I had left school that he had regularly serviced the head mistress herself a devout Christian lesbian of over sixty years.

Of course Henri, that was his name couldn't sustain the demands made on him, and at the age of forty two he had a massive heart attack whilst fucking the headmistress Miss Henderson up the arse. and from what I was told by the school secretary another dear friend whose weird fantasies taught me a lot about sex, but that's another story.

Anyway she told me that she couldn't get his dick out of her bum. Something about a death spasm, well they were carried out locked together on a stretcher from the school and taken to a private hospital that her brother ran.

I heard that she retired soon after."

"So how did you meet your husband? Tim isn't it."

"Soups ready, do you want it out there or in the kitchen?" Mary's voice came through the open window.

Jayne glanced at Janice who shivered.

"I thing we'll come inside." Janice called back. "Jayne's nipples are about to poke through her dress." The warmth of the kitchen was inviting and the soup delicious."

"You were about to tell me how you met Tim." Jayne said wiping her bowl clean with the last of her bread.

"That's no great story, a friend and I were in a pub in London, and there was this group of what we leant later doctors who had graduated a few days earlier.

Well they were pretty drunk and playing a game where each one had to write down three things about themselves that the others couldn't ever have known about them.

One had to be completely true, the other, had to be something they really wanted to do in their lifetime, and the third had to be a complete untruth.

Jennifer that was my friend at the time and I were sitting at the next table, eavesdropping you might say, and well we took something of an interest.

Anyway I can't remember what all the answers were except one, and Tim wrote that he wanted to marry the dark haired girl on the next table. Well as Jennie had blonde hair, I knew he was referring to me. And that's how it all started, and Tim knew from that day that I was totally bi-sexual and has been fine with it for the past fifteen years.

Hardly a Mills and Boon story is it?" Janice said smiling and placing her hands on the legs of the woman on either side of her.

"Sounds rather lovely and good way to learn about someone you hardly know." Jayne said placing her hand on top of Janice's.

"What do you say about us three playing the same game?" Mary said reaching across to the drawer where she withdrew a notepad and a bundle of pens tied with an elastic band.

"Why not?" Janice agreed it might be fun, but no cheating.

"As if we would." Mary laughed.

Right in any order. One thing about your life that is true, another that you would love to happen. And three a downright lie. Now try to make the lie believable otherwise it rather spoils the game; and please be as honest and outrageous as you want, in fact the more outrageous the better."

The supposedly three simple tasks took over fifteen minutes to complete with numerous crossing outs.

Finally they pushed the papers over to Mary who had assumed leadership of the game.

"Janice first I will read them all out and then we can take them one at a time. "

Mary read out.

Janice; I want to be sitting naked on a man's cock while riding a horse, with me facing him of course.

Mary and Jayne smiled at the image their minds created.

Number two: To be fucked while bending over the church altar. And the third one; to have at least six women using my body for anything and everything.

Both Mary and Jayne easily guessed the lie but pondered on the other two.

"Don't answer yet let's read them all out first?" Mary said. Now lets see what Jayne has written?" she said trying desperately to suppress a fit of laughter.

To watch a man with a huge cock fucking two women." "Well that sounds interesting." Mary said her face flushing slightly.

Number two is to watch while Jonas is raped by two women with a butternut squash."

All three women bust into fits of laughter

"Brilliant." Janice said trying to remove the image from her mind.

"Thirdly to get the new vicar to fuck me within the six weeks."

"Well that's an easy one." Janice grinned.

Now me." Mary said smiling. "To meet another man like Teddy."

Even as she read it out the others immediately put it down as the lie.

"To be screwed up my arse by the biggest real cock I can find. And last but not least; to share one virile man with my two friends." "Right who's shall we decide on first. Mary concluded.

"I think we should do Mary first" Janice said. "And for me replacing Teddy well that's a lie."

"I think so too." agreed Jayne.

Mary smiled knowingly; no one could ever replace her Teddy.

"Her bum has to be her greatest desire, but the sharing with her friends is more like the unselfish Mary I know." Janice smiled. "But no I am going with her arsehole."

"I think it's the friends?" Jayne said.

"Janice is right." Mary said "Teddy wasn't the biggest of men in that department, but he satisfied me back then, but now I would love to feel something that give both pain and pleasure at the same time, and now you know my secrets desires. So Janice it's your turn next. We shall leave the newcomer till last."

"For me Janice you are about as transparent as a newly cleaned window, talking of which Eric will be here all next week cleaning the windows so be warned, no fingering each other while he's around that little bastard misses nothing." Mary grinned.

"Now Janice the church altar, I am surprised I really thought you were an atheist. I mean you only ever go to church for weddings and funerals. But I now recall you mentioning years ago that your parents were Quakers weren't they?"

"Yes and let's not go into my beliefs, and you are right the alter thing is a definite no-no for me."

"So that leaves the horse which I find rather bizarre, but then again bizarre does fit you sometimes, but I can see from Jayne's face that the six women is your dearest desire."

"Or more if they are available." Janice sniggered.

"So now we have Jayne our comedienne to contend with. It's where do we put the butternut squash; first or second?"

"I rather think Jayne would prefer we put it up his arsehole." Janice howled again the thought of the look on the vicar's face as she and Jayne rammed it inside him.

"You idiot." Mary laughed. "But watching two women and a man perform. I can somehow visualize Jayne wanting to do that, I get the impression she could be something of a voyeur."

"No I prefer the butternut squash as her first choice." Janice laughed again tears trickled down her face.

"So we are both agreed that the new vicar is the definite none starter."

"Well Jayne, how did we do?" Janice asked.

"At this moment in time I want my pleasures first and revenge takes second place. And yes the vicar thing, was all I could come up with." Jayne said smiling.

"Ah but what if you were one of the two women with the single man instead of just watching?" Janice said conspiratorially.

Jayne felt the colour rise up her neck.

"Sounds like that might work." she replied recalling the same event happening in the book.

It was the thought of the book that triggered her thought.

"Oh shit" she exclaimed. "I have left the book on the kitchen table, and the doors not locked what if this new vicar comes early and finds it."

"Calm down, what time is he due?" Mary asked.

"I don't know around six I think?"

68

"Well its only just after three so it's unlikely he will be three hours early, not with the way the trains run around here anyway. I assume he will be coming by train?" Mary added.

"I have no idea; I don't even know his name. Jonas couldn't remember it and went off is such a rush, and I didn't bother to ask I was just glad he was going."

Anyone for more soup there's plenty left?"

Both women nodded and Mary put it back on the stove to warm.

"Fancy free and nowhere to go." Janice said "So what about a trip to Salisbury. I heard of a little sex shop behind the cathedral, that once word gets around could easily be closed soon; you know what a virtuous lot the councilors are in that fair city. How about we take a day out and maybe do a bit of shopping tomorrow. I know Jayne will want to get away from her onerous guest, and I really want to buy some of these toys. I know one can get them online, but they need a name and address to send them and well I would rather avoid going down that route."

"I don't know what if we were to bump into some we know, coming out of such a place, I mean what would people say?" Jayne replied warily.

"Not a problem, leave it to me by the time I have finished with the three of us we won't even recognize each other. So girls if I can make you pass muster are you on for a fun day out. I am sure Jayne will welcome the opportunity to refurbish her wardrobe. While the cats away and all that?"

"Yes please." Jayne said clapping her hands "But are you sure you can make us unrecognizable in a nice way." She added.

"Trust me now finish your soup, I have some errands to run, and you have a dirty book to hide before the new vicar brings damnation down on your beautiful head. Now be at my house at eight sharp. Tim leaves for surgery at a quarter to, so we shall be alone. Now until tomorrow and don't do anything I wouldn't." Janice laughed as she scurried out and seconds later the sound of her new BMW roared across the loose gravel scattering it across the neatly trimmed lawn.

"I suppose I ought to get back in case my guest turns up early, I should at least be there to welcome him; after all it's not his fault he has been dumped on us at the last minute." Janice said smiling into Mary's eyes.
"I understand my dear." Mary replied.
"Kiss me before I go?" Jayne asked." You really do make me feel special when you kiss me."
A tear trickled down the older woman's face.
"That's what Teddy used to say." She sad pulling Jayne's face onto her own. Their parted lips paused as the exchanged breath before Mary's nimble tongue brushed along the outside of Jayne's lips before tracing the insides, and onto engaging with Jayne's own equally erotic tongue.
"She felt Mary's fingers tracing up her legs lifting the short skirt higher until her hand cupped her pubic mound with the tip of her forefinger brushing her now swollen love button.
Still kissing passionately Jayne's own hand brushing through the deep mattress of curled pubic hair until her fingers tugged gently on Mary's hanging labia lips before she eased he fingers into the wet hole.
Mary's lags parted wider and Jayne remembering the game they had played pushed her fingers beyond the vagina and located the small wrinkled hole.

With her fingers still moist she pressed her forefinger against the center of her arsehole and was amazed how easily it slid inside.

"Let me sit on the table." Mary gasped shuffling herself towards the edge of the table.

With one foot on the chair Mary levered herself onto the kitchen table and raised her spread legs so Jayne's finger could penetrate her bottom fully.

"Oh yes please; do it slowly, that feels so nice, do you mind if I just come like this?" Mary asked her own fingers pressing against her open vagina.

"Yes just come when you are ready nice and slow." Jayne whispered as her finger reamed around the inner walls of Mary bottom brushing the already sensitized nerves that made her hole so aroused.

Mary shuddered several times as a ripple of orgasms brought the satisfaction her body demanded.

Chapter 7

Jayne hurried up the drive and into the kitchen and breathed a sigh of relief to see the book laying on the table exactly where she had abandoned in earlier in her haste to get to the Grange.

She swept it up and hurried upstairs and returned it to its hiding place beneath the mattress.

Knowing it safe from detection she returned to the kitchen. And as much from force of habit rather than design she began making dinner.

She peeled and diced the potatoes, and with the chopped leeks and onions, with salt and pepper she put them onto boil, she would add the Bockwurst later with the crème fresh.

The spare bedroom was next on her agenda and she retrieved fresh linen from the airing cupboard and stripping the unused bedding from the mattress she flung the window wide open, and lit the two firelighters in the corner fire grate. She piled on half a bucket of coal, with the draft from the open window the coals caught fast.

She quickly remade the bed and fluffed up the duck down duvet.

She glanced at the wall clock and saw that it was almost a quarter to six.

Closing the window and placing the wire guard around the open fire, she returned to the kitchen.

She mashed the potatoes leeks and onions and added a knob of butter and the tub of crème fresh and blended them together.

She then chopped up the eight Bockwurst and dropped them into the thick soupy mash.

Sitting down she remembered that underneath her dress she was naked, and as she headed towards the stairs she heard a car pull onto the drive.

Glancing through the net curtains she saw it was Reg Trumble's car which he ran as the local taxi.

"No time to get my knickers and bra on now." She muttered to herself reaching behind her for her long cardigan which she hurriedly slipped her bare arms into.

In the early darkness she couldn't make the features of the man that squeezed his way out of the front passenger seat.

"Unusual." She thought Reg was very fastidious about passengers sitting in the rear.

"She could see that he was a tall well built man, and the words 'brick shithouse' flashed through her mind.

However he wore a hooded jacket and Reg was struggling to lift out what looked like a large military holdall from the boot.

The man grabbed the holdall handles and easily lifted it clear.

She watched as the passenger pressed several notes into Reg's protesting hand.

Another unusual event she thought recalling the few times she had used the taxi; it was often hard to get Reg to give change at the best of times.

Jayne suddenly felt a wave of nervousness flood over her, and as the man headed towards the door Jayne's waited nervously for his knock.

At the first tap she yanked the door open, and a tall wide grinned face beamed at her.

"Mrs. Beech, or would that be your mother?" his voice was strong yet soft with only the faintest of Belfast Irish accent to be heard.

"It's Jayne and my mother has been dead a long time now." Jayne smiled knowing she liked this young man the instant he smiled at her.

"And I know this has to be a daft question, but I have to assume that you are the new vicar that is standing in for my husband for the next six weeks?"

"I am indeed. Jayne." he added. "And I should add its pretty cold out here, and your cooking smells divine."

"Oh dear I am so terribly sorry. Yes please come in. I really don't know what I was thinking, only to tell the truth, you are nothing at all that I was expecting, and please don't take this the wrong way but dressed like that you have to be the most unlikely candidate to be a clergyman."

"That Jayne is about the nicest thing you could have said to me. By the way the name's Rory. Rory Killeen originally from Belfast, but that was many years ago, now I am from too many places to mention."

"Please put you bag down, I will show you to your room later, but first come and get warm. I hope you like Bockwurst…"

"In potato soup with leeks and onions." He asked his eyes swinging towards the bubbling pot.

"And crème fresh and butter." Jayne added enjoying the new vicars company even more.

"Brings back my memories of Germany, and when we hadn't cream or anything else soft cheese used to give

74

it a slightly different twist. But yes Bockwurst will do me fine."

Jayne managed just one small bowl while Rory finished of the rest.

"I hope you don't mind, only airplane food just doesn't hit the spot like that." he said leaning back in his chair."

"Tea, coffee or a large single malt whisky." Jayne asked.

"As the host I believe you should choose, but hot drinks tend to give me indigestion after a good meal." He replied the mischievous smile seemed embedded in his square rugged face with its dark shadow of unshaven stubble. His thick dark almost black hair was tousled, and in need of cutting.

But it was his dark brown eyes that seemed capable of almost anything.

"You are studying me, what is it you are expecting to find?" he asked curiously. "I had the horns removed just yesterday, and the forked tail is to be my next surgery."

"Sorry, I didn't mean to stare, only my friends and I tried to picture you with just the knowledge that you were a mature student who only recently graduated and you were arriving from Belfast, and you are absolute nothing at all what we depicted."

"I see so you were expecting an aged old bogtrotter that smelt of stale cigarettes and beer." He laughed.

"Not the cigarettes or beer, we hadn't quite got that far, but I suppose the first bit came close. You really must think we are awful?"

"Indeed I do not, you see you were not exactly what my own imagination conjured up and expected to open the door, and for a moment I really did think that you might be the vicar's unmarried daughter, that was until I realized that such a beauty as yourself could not be unmarried. And now I see that I have embarrassed you, which was something I had certainly not intended to do, and for someone I have only met an hour ago I am talking far more than I usually do. And you mentioned a single malt?"

"Of course I am sorry Mr...."

"Rory please, Mr. Killeen was me father and he's no longer with us, and every time someone mentions his name I get terrible sad." He chuckled knowing she believed little of his blarney.

"Whisky, yes indeed I am sure Jonas, that's my husband wouldn't mind sharing, an act of Christian charity, and besides what the eyes don't see the heart will not greave for." Jayne said opening the cabinet a bringing the almost full bottle of Jameson's single malt whisky with her fingers inside two lead crystal glasses.

"Jameson's single malt from Waterford crystal glasses; indeed Jayne your husband is a man after my own heart."

"Don't worry he has several cases in the cellar, for emergencies and as I see it every time one is in need of pleasure then its an emergency." Jayne suddenly felt an abandonment that added to the one she had experienced when Jonas had left only this morning, she felt as if it had been a week.

"You sound as if you to have an Irish heart beating in your chest." He said his eyes resting on her opened cardigan and her clearly visible protrusions of her rounded breasts.

He dragged his eyes away, feeling warmth creeping up his groin.

"Will you not join me, and we can toast to our new relationship; to which it now appears will be far more acceptable to the one either of us was expecting.

Jayne sipped the smooth silky liquid feeling its warmth settle in her full stomach.

"You started to tell me earlier exactly what you thought I would be like, when I opened the door, before you sneakily diverted my attention with your exquisite Irish charm. So let's hear exactly what you thought would open the door.

"Praise god you are a desperate woman who wants to know everything."

He said before taking a mouthful and allowing it to rest a moment in his mouth before letting it slide down his throat.

"Well you are a good five inches taller, than I estimated. and at least fifty pounds lighter. The grey hair pulled back into a bun, has magically been exchanged to one of a lovely colour; of which I have no idea what that colour is called only to say it looks a mite reddish and very natural."

"It is natural, and it's called auburn, and no it doesn't come off at night." Jayne said as seriously as she could manage.

"And what else, have you failed to mention. The varicose veins, warts, my cross eyes, knock knees or bow legs."

"Now you're making fun of me." Rory smiled. "But I suppose I deserve it." Rory face took on a hurt expression, which Jayne could no longer control her mirth.

"Come on let's adjourn to the lounge, and bring the bottle with you. I really feel like celebrating if only that neither of us lived up to expectations." Jayne said not wishing to go into the details she, Janice and Mary had speculated on.

Rory threw the remainder of the coals onto the fire and poured Jayne another half a glass of the amber nectar.

"Do you drink much?" Rory asked seeing a glaze already appearing over her face.

"Only when I'm pissed. Oh my god did I really say that. I didn't mean for that to come out the way it did. Please forgive me. I only ever cuss when I have drunk too much or am totally angry, which isn't often on either occasion."

"Pleased to hear it, I wouldn't want to be accused of leading down any other path than the one of righteousness."

"You know Rory, and I admit I like that name. " Jayne's voice was beginning to slur even more.

"Rory leant across the small coffee table and pulled her almost empty glass away from her.

"Yes, apparently it was my grandfather's name, but he was finished with so they gave it me."

"You have an answer for everything, but what I don't understand, and yes in three hours you have got me drunker than... "She almost said two days ago but managed to stop the words in time.

"...since I don't know when. But please tell me, what on earth made you decide to become a clergyman. You seem capable of being anything, and yet you seem willing to settle for a country parish or maybe an inner city one, whichever one is irrelevant, and somehow I find it difficult to understand."

"It's not that difficult. I have done a great many things in my life that have not always been beneficial to mankind. I joined the army as a sixteen year old, and later went to many places where men like me were

78

needed. Well that's what the politicians said. From Iraq to Afghanistan, and a number of other places where we weren't technically supposed to be and I saw too many terrible sights that one day, just became one too many and I left the army and retreated into a world where I could find peace. Buddhism seemed to be the one faith that shied away from war and so I spent several years in the Thailand where I studied its religion, until I realized that that too was not for me. But I liked the country and the people, and to survive I took up writing, not about the conflicts but rather about the many people I had met and learnt about that preferred the art of making love to that of making war.

"Another drink?" Jayne asked her wavering hand trying to refill his glass.

"No I think we have both had enough, and I am telling you this in the hope you will probably forget most of it by morning, and I at least will have a clear conscience."

Jayne smiled inanely at him, knowing he was probably right, but for now she just wanted to hear the sound of his voice.

"So what books did you write and did you get them published."

They were published by a small printing house in Bangkok, and I made enough money to survive and I managed to save enough for a flight home. That was over five years ago now, and now I finally have got my head and act together, thanks to the church it gave me somewhere to think and recover. My head was in a pretty awful state.

"What were your books about; you said they were about love and it being the opposite to war."

"Well to be honest they were written for a special sort of reader, and thankfully I had the sense to use an alias that couldn't be traced back to me."

"Well what was it?" Jayne asked again "Maybe I had heard of you."

"I sincerely hope not in fact I most definitely I hope not." Rory chuckled.

"So if they weren't published over here what have you got to loose by telling me." Jayne slurring voice almost insisted.

"First of all if you do ever come across one, which I very much doubt, please do not read it, you are far too nice a person, and I know I am making excuses but they were written to allow me to survive and to get back to the UK."

"How on earth will I know I have come across one if I don't know what name you wrote under?" Jayne felt her question made sense. "And did you get a kick out of writing as well?" Jayne added questioningly.

"I suppose so. Well all I retained was my initials, so if you come across a book whose author has the initial RK please avoid it."

"RK that's your initials." Jayne sounded confused.

"Yes of course Rory Killeen, RK." Rory laughed "Somehow one does try to hold onto ones work no matter how it's received. So yes I did use my initials but not my name or anything close."

He said cautiously.

Jayne thought of the book hidden beneath the mattress, and paled as she imagined Rory being the author.

"Are you alright Jayne you have gone deathly pale." Do you feel sick; maybe you have drunk too much? Rory said concerned.

"RK?" Jayne mumbled her colour returning and devilish grin began to spread across her face.

"RK." She repeated it, again remembered the book beneath her mattress.

Realization was slow coming to Rory and Jayne repeating his initials added to the realization that his initials triggered something inside her brain.

"Maybe we should leave it right here." Jayne said her voice no longer slurred, but the grin on her face kept getting wider, and she had to force herself to keep a straight face.

"Dare I ask him?" the unspoken words raced through her mind. "And what if I am wrong and he has maybe read the books, then I will look a complete idiot and I will never be able to look him in the face; and if I am right Rory will certainly be terribly embarrassed?"

"So Rory lets make a pact."

"A pact?"

"Yes a pact, not to pry too deeply into each others lives; it can only lead to problems."

"I am game if you are." He said feeling that she knew more than she wanted to admit about his books. But thinking and knowing were poles apart and they had only just met.

"Right just another small one, then I am off to bed." Jayne said "Then I will show you your room, it should be warm, I had a fire going today and I changed the sheets. There is a wardrobe and plenty of drawer space, any washing you want doing just dump it in the laundry basket marked men in the bathroom. And in the morning I shall be out early well if quarter to eight is early.

All the church paperwork is in the study and I almost forgot you have a wedding to officiate on Saturday at ten in the morning, and well Sundays you should know all about."

Jayne downed what had been left in her glass. "Leave the dishes I can do them before I go out in the morning. Grab your bag and follow me." She ordered."

"Yes ma'am." Rory said grinning. Holding onto Jayne's arm to steady her.

Weaving slightly Jayne led the way up the stairs, and the absence of a panty line was not lost on the flowing Rory.

"That's your room, so I might see you in the morning if not I will be home for dinner, Goodnight Rory and it really is nice to meet you and I am sure we will get on fine, and now half an hour with my book and the sleep. Oh the bathrooms down the end of the passage" She added.

"Goodnight Jayne and the same goes for me. What book are you reading?"

"Just something by… Er Rita Kennedy." She blurted out. "Mills and Boon stuff." She said emphasizing the name and a curious smile crept across her inebriated face.

It wasn't until he closed the door that he realized that she had used the RK initials again. He could see that unless he was very careful it could become an issue. It had been that hint of a smile when she put the emphasis on the author's name which hadn't registered until now.

And he dumped his holdall on the floor and caste a quizzical eye towards the closed door.

He shook his head, there was no way she could have gotten her hands on one of his books, as far as he was aware the publisher distributed then to Hong Kong

Singapore and Australia and New Zealand and sales weren't nothing to write home about.

No he was just being paranoid and Jayne was just trying to pull his chain.

He chuckled to himself. "Well we can both play that game."

The silence in the house was complete not even the usual night sounds seemed to penetrate the inside of the house.

Rory suddenly realized he needed to use the toilet he had drunk far more than he had become accustomed to in the student lodgings.

He eased the door open and crept down the landing in his stocking feet.

Stopping as faint sounds of Jayne moaning filtered through the thick door.

For a moment he thought she might be in pain until her heard her heavy breathing.

Rory slipped back to his room and opened and closed the door without attempting to hide the noise.

The noise coming from Jayne's room had ceased and Rory continued onto the toilet a confused look fixed firmly on his face.

Chapter 8

Jayne woke to the aroma of bacon and faint sounds coming from the kitchen.

She glanced at the alarm clock and saw that it was about to go off in two minutes.

She pressed the stop button and slid out of bed.

She was naked her nightgown still lay across the back of the chair.

Religious Desires lay open on the pillow.

She picked it up and turned it over at the bottom of the back cover in small print was written "Published in Bangkok by Phu Boong Ltd. All rights reserved."

"Gotcha." She whispered before slipping it beneath the mattress. She quickly showered and cleaned her teeth three times to remove the fur from inside her mouth before dressing and ensuring that she chose a thicker brassiere and her Marks and Spencer knickers.

She made her way down the stairs as the smiling Rory dressed in a fresh check shirt and denim jeans, was cracking eggs into the frying pan.

"Good morning, one or two?" he asked.

"One or two what?" she asked.

He held up the egg for her to see.

"One please, and this is a wonderful surprise. I can't remember when someone else last cooked for breakfast me."

Jayne noticed that all the dishes from the previous evenings meal had been washed dried and put away.

"You have been busy what time did you get up?"

"Five o clock as always, and completed my three mile run, and decided to tidy up; now sit yourself down." He said smiling into her eyes as he slid the loaded plate in front of her.

"My I hope you don't expect me to eat this much every morning, I will be huge by the time Jonas gets back." Jayne said tucking into the large breakfast.

"If you are to spend the day shopping with your friends then you need something to sustain you, or perhaps you should get up at five o clock and join me in my early morning run, then you would be able to eat a heart breakfast afterwards.

"Oh no, five in the morning for me; I love my bed in the mornings and anyway I am far too old to take up running."

"Old, only in the mind perhaps, but even so I doubt that after last night. What age are you and I know it's not the done thing to question the age of a woman, but you brought it up; so let me see, you said you had been married for twenty years, and how old were you when your Jonas swept you off your feet, eighteen at the most.

"Twenty one almost, so now you know how old I am and you are what? I can't remember what dates of your wars, but you joined the army at sixteen and a rough guess at least twelve years in the army, lets say three maybe four years in Thailand and another three at the Christian college comes to around thirty four or five maybe.

"Close and thank I you for those three years."

"So you're just two years younger than I am; but that does not mean I am getting up a five in the morning to run three miles,"

"Well I agree it's not as if you need to tone up your body, it looks in great shape to me, anyway coffee's ready when you are." he said reaching for the pot.

"Black no sugar, just how it is supposed to be drunk." he said.

"By the way did you enjoy your Rose Kennedy last night?

"Rose who?" Jayne queried.

"Rose Kennedy your Mills and Boon novel." Rory read the name slowly deliberately changing the authors name she had given him lat night, from Rita to Rose.

Realization dawned on her and she felt colour rising up her neck.

"Yes; well no, not really Ms Connelly can get rather same old, same old, if you know what I mean."

"You mean Kennedy?" Rory smiled knowingly.

"Yes of course, there are so many of them, it does get a little confusing; you would think she would make up a name that was somehow original and unforgettable like Ruby Kettle wouldn't you?"

"Would seem to make sense, one needs a distinctive name sometimes, easier for the reader to find other books written by the same author; but I thought you were supposed to be going out at a quarter to eight, and its almost ten to."

"Oh shi... Sugar. She swore. "That's you keeping me talking. Well thank you again for breakfast and everything; bye for now, you know where everything is so just make this your home, and I will see you later, not sure what time but, it should be before six."

"Begone woman and don't forget your coat." he said standing up and stood watching through the kitchen window as she hurried down the drive.

"Well what's he like?" Janice and Mary chorused as she entered Janice's house.

"Please let me take my coat off?" Jayne said smiling.

"Well?" Janice urged.

"Exactly as we predicted. Short, weedy, balding on top, and about as Irish as they come, and he smells of B.O." Jayne said trying to keep her face straight.

"Liar, liar, liar." Janice howled back at her.

Under the onslaught Jayne couldn't restrain herself any longer and she burst out laughing.

"I knew you were fibbing. Tim and I nipped into the Crowne for a meal, and Reg was in there telling everyone about the new vicar, apparently Reg knew him from his own time in the army, and his description was more about the man himself, rather than what he looked like, but his description and that disgusting great fib you told just do not go together. So unless you want to end up a frustrated old woman, tell us everything. You can talk while I change you into someone else."

Mary and Jayne followed her up the stairs into the second of the large bedrooms that doubled as Janice's wardrobe.

"Goodness me, are you opening your own boutique." Jayne exclaimed at the array of designer dresses along with several rails of what is described as retro clothes.

"These are not all mine, well yes they are mine but not ones I wear.

Several years ago I practically ran the Devises amateur dramatic society, and well when the old Adelphi theatre became a supermarket we sort of dissolved, and I ended up with all of the costumes and accessories. Anyway Jayne lets strip you off and start with a blank canvas as they say.

Before Jayne could object her dress was hauled up over her head and her uninspiring M&S underwear was discarded with the undressors sniggering.

"I only wore those because…"

"You didn't want your lodger ogling your nipples." Mary laughed, as Jayne nodded.

"Yes we assumed that we aren't as daft as we look." Janice said pulling the nude Jayne into the chair facing the window.

"I need the natural light." Janice fibbed she didn't want Jayne seeing herself until Janice had completed her transformation.

"So, what's he like then?" Janice urged as she retrieved a long blonde wig from the polystyrene head.

Jayne described his physical features in great deal even to the several scars his violent life had left him with."

"You certainly didn't miss much for just one evening." Janice grinned.

"Any other scars anywhere else?" she asked teasing the natural blond hairs of the wig into an expertly coiffured style.

"I expect so, but as they were not on display I have no idea." Jayne countered.

"So that's what he looks like, and he sounds exceptionally edible." Janice whispered leeringly.

"But what's he like as a person, is he the shy retiring type or what?" Janice probed.

Jayne suddenly laughed and received a gentle tap on her bare shoulder and told to stay still.

"Far from shy and retiring in fact I would say the complete opposite."

"You mean like your bogus description when you arrived." Mary chipped in.

"Yes sorry about that, but Rory that's his name by the way. Rory Killeen. He is incredibly amusing, and from what I learnt about him he has lived what I would say, was an exciting and at times dangerous sort of life, but I gather he has lived through some rather dark moments in his life, and he is certainly very nice. I woke this morning to a clean kitchen and a whopping great breakfast of about everything you could get onto one plate." Jayne stared dreamily towards the ceiling.

"Details Jayne, tell us details?" Janice urged patting the hair into place.

"Now for your make-up." She said pulling a tiered make up trolley towards her and another chair for herself.

"There are no details as you call them we just spent a pleasant evening, drinking Jonas's single malt, and talking, and to be honest, I drank rather too much of the amber nectar." Jayne managed to say before Janice applied the sophisticated red lipstick and pressed a folded tissue between her lips.

"You mean the devil got you pissed, and probably had his evil way with you?" Mary giggled uncontrollably falling backwards onto the bed."

"And you too drunk to remember. That really is a bummer." Janice added trying to keep her hand steady as she drew the eyeliner around Jayne's wide open eyes.

"Keep still or I might poke you in the eye." Janice admonished the protesting Jayne.

"Mary get of your bottom and help put these stocking on her." Janice said stretching her hand towards the struggling Mary who was still trying to control her giggling.

Finally with both stocking up to below the knees Jayne stood up and the kneeling Mary's vision was filled with the dark auburn curls of Jane's Veneris Mons , easing her legs far enough apart her eyes easily picked out the closed labia.

"Mary for goodness sake get your face out of her fanny, we haven't time for your lecherous behavior." Janice said curtly.

"Mary poked her tongue out at her and smoothed the dark pull-up stocking into place allowing her fingers to briefly brush Jayne's labia lips.

"Panties next." Janice said throwing a pair of the briefest red lace knickers Jayne had ever seen to the still kneeling and leching Mary.

With Jayne's fanny settled into a pair of Janice's knickers Mary struggled to her feet."

"Step in." Janice said holding the 'just above the knee length' red dress open.

Janice eased it up over Jayne's bottom and waited while Jayne slipped her hands into the arm openings.

Janice eased Jayne's unfettered breasts into the perfect fitting dress and slid the zipper up the back.

"Six or six and a half?" Janice asked holding up two similar black high heeled shoes.

"The larger one." Jayne replied feeling that she should have shoes that fitted instead of allowing her vanity over the size of her to feet dictate comfort.

"Right just the accessories left to do. No pierced ears so its clip-on's." she murmured to herself as she rooted through a huge four tiered jewelry box.

"These will do fine she said.

"Black onyx with that red dress is perfect." She said clipping the small earrings into place and snapping the matching necklace around Jayne's throat. "One last thing." she added spraying several puffs of her Chanel no 5 in front of Jayne. "Walk through the mist." she said pulling at Jayne's hand. "And now Miss Dora Duck the lady who loves to…"

"Drink Coffee." Mary finished off for her.

"Precisely." Janice ginned. "And now darling to the mirror." Janice and Mary led her through into the master bedroom where the curved arrangement of mirrors that covered the one wall allowed Jayne to view her front and profile in six different mirrors simultaneously.

Jayne squealed at the vision of the stranger who stared back at her.

"That can't be me, she looks like a film star." She gasped disbelievingly lifting her hand to her mouth and seeing the image to the front and sides of her doing the same, and then she noticed the huge mirror behind the low headboard of the bed that stretched to the ceiling that had been cunningly angled for a full rear view, allowed her to see her behind.

"Does this make my arse look big?" she asked nervously.

Both Mary and Janice burst into peals of laughter.

"Of course not but it certainly looks terribly sexual. But enough I still have Mary and myself to do, and time is a wasting as they say."

The black three-quarter length real mink coat that Janice had placed over Jayne's shoulder came from the theatrical retro rail.

Real fur being frowned on in these enlightened days, but now old enough for the vast majority of fashion conscious people to have forgotten what real fur looked and felt like.

Janice had altered her own appearance in clothing almost the opposite of Jayne's.

Jet black hair, black dress red jewelry, and a matching red swagger coat as well as red high heeled shoes and Gucci handbag.

She had deliberately darkened her eyes with make up giving her a slight sinister appearance.

Mary had demanded a much calmer look as she called it.

The highlighted wig and Janice's expertise with the make up made Mary look at least ten years younger. However the vee necked emerald green silk dress revealed just enough of her ample charms that Janice knew would probably draw the eyes of the younger men away from her own and Jayne's well positioned breasts.

Mary was equally amazed at her own transformation when Janice allowed her into the master bedroom.

The matching green accompaniments, and wide black belt, and her lower heeled black patent leather shoes were about as perfect as Mary could have hoped, and silently wished that Teddy could see her now.

An hour later the three completely different women made their way into the garage, and climbed into Janice's BMW. Its tinted windows hiding them from view of any villagers they might pass, who would probably call the police believing that the Doctors wife's car was being stolen.

Janice drove to the empty top floor of the multi story car park, and they descended to the ground floor in the urine smelling lift.

"Shall we have a coffee first before we shop?" Mary asked hopefully the excitement of the morning was not something she was used to.

"Wonderful suggestion my dear." Janice replied in a superior accented voice.

"Just working in character sometimes ones voice is as revealing as a photograph."

Jayne smiled at Mary while Janice surged ahead to find a table in the Costa coffee outlet of the departments store

When they caught up with her she was busy instructing the young waiter on how to wipe the table down correctly, her accent drawing several smiles from the other occupied tables.

As Jayne edged her way past one table she overheard a pimply long haired student.

"Toffee nosed cow, I bet she hasn't done a days work in her entire life."

It was only when she sat down did she realize that the scruffy student was the youngest son of the Olde Crowne landlord.

"See spotty on the table by the entrance..." Jayne said.

"Who? Oh you mean the landlord's son Terrance?" Janice said haughtily.

"Well he thinks you are a toffee nosed snob who doesn't know what work is." Jayne sniggered.

"See I told you we wouldn't be recognized." Janice said smugly.

After three hours of constant shopping all three women admitted they were exhausted.

"Shall we make our way back to the sex shop and then call it a day?" Janice said "My feet are killing me."

Both Mary and Jayne thankfully agreed and with the cathedral in sight they strode purposely along the High Street with aching bag laden arms.

"Oh my god it's that pompous old windbag Fortescue. The head and self righteous judge of the women's guild, and poor little Denis, see how he trots behind like a lap dog.

"Young lady." The high-pitched whining voice echoed across the whole street. "Yes you in the fur coat."

Jayne suddenly felt herself blushing.

"That coat is real fur, and I know about such things I don't know how…"

She stopped in mid sentence as Janice's hand gripped her arm above the elbow, and she leant towards the surprised woman, and whispered just loud enough for those closest to be able to hear in what Jayne and Mary took to be a broad east London accent.

"If you dare say another fucking word, you frustrated old cow, I will kick you cunt up into your mouth and dump you on you bleedin arse in the middle of the road and take a photograph of you with my phone and I guarantee it will be on the front page of every newspaper by the morning now bleedin apologize and fuck off."

Cicely Fortescue's legs wobbled and she struggled to breathe; her terrified eyes bulged from their sockets. But as Janice nails dug deeper into her flabby upper arm she managed to gasp her sincere apology for mistaking the young lady's coat."

"Thank you my dear and how magnanimous it was of you to accede to the truth." Janice's voice had returned to her upper class accent.

As they strode away the flustered shaken woman took a small bottle of smelling salts from her cavernous bag

94

and held them to her nose while Dennis winked at the women and hid his smile behind his hand.

"Played an East End tart a few years ago." Janice enlightened her two open mouthed friends.

"I just hope she never finds out who we really are?" Mary said. "She is a hell of a vindictive woman."

"What would you have done if she had called your bluff?" Jayne's asked.

"Who said anything about bluffing?" Janice said her voice deadly serious, as she swung her state of the art mobile phone on its cord.

"I did a course on karate, and I do happen to know a journalist who would kill for such a picture."

"There's even more to you than I know." Mary said linking arms with the two younger women.

The sex shop had little of real interest in it small window, probably trying to sit as far under the radar, so that the notoriously moral city council might miss the significance of his wares.

The small bell tinkled as they entered, and again Jayne averted her head and whispered.

"Its Eric, what on earth can he be doing here?"

"Same as us probably looking for that little something to brighten his boring life."

"But according to that notice above his head he is in the gay section." Jayne whispered.

"Indeed he is." Janice said easing her way across the cluttered shop and glancing down the narrow aisle she could see that Reg was engrossed in an explicit magazine of men buggering other men.

Janice managed to get off three pictures before Reg became conscious that he was being watched, and in a flash he had dropped the magazine and barged past the smirking Janice and disappeared into the darkening early evening.

"Let the little shit ever try gossiping again." Janice laughed.

Twenty minutes later with another bag full of sexual purchases they made their way slowly back to the car park.

They giggled like naughty schoolgirls during the hour long drive back to Janice's.

Still giggling and loaded with their bags of purchases the barged their way into the lounge.

"Who the bloody hell are you?" Tim's angry but extremity nervous voice filled the room.

The swung round to see him framed in the doorway a marble rolling pin in his hand.

Janice was the first to start laughing, followed by Mary while Jayne backed nervously against the wall."

"Janice? Is that you?" Tim asked incredulously raising the rolling pin still not connecting his wife's distinctive laugh to the image that confronted him.

With tears of laughter destroying her make up, she pulled the black wig from her head.

"Of course it me you twit now put that rolling pin down before you hurt yourself."

"Ok so it is you, but who are your friends." Tim asked convinced but still confused.

"Mary, meet Tim my husband." She said lifting Mary's highlighted hair piece from her head and rubbing her fingers through her friend's hair to reveal her identity, again Tim's jaw dropped in amazement.

"And last, but by no means least I want you to meet Jayne the wife of our absent vicar."

Tim's jaw dropped even further as he stared open mouthed as Jayne eased the blonde wig from her head and shaking her head to loosen her own hair.

"Oh my giddy aunt; I would never ever have guessed. But?" his voice took on a serious note.

"What on earth have three you been up to? I expect crazy from Janice, but Mary, and of all people Jayne. I just know that whatever you have been indulging yourselves in the whole idea must have come from Janice, but why?"

Mary and Jayne avoided Time's gaze wondering what sort of explanation he would believe that would cover their behavior; if indeed they could have thought of one.

Jayne knew that Tim would not accept a sudden triple mental aberration, but that was all she could come up with.

"I'll explain later." Janice said to the relief of her friends. "And as a matter of interest what are you doing home at this time; and where is your car? I hope you are not snooping on me?"

"Of course I am not snooping what do you take me for? And no please don't answer that. My car wouldn't start, and I knew you were going shopping but I assumed you would have been back by now as I was going to borrow yours."

"Phone; Durr." Janice said holding her phone for him to see.

"It's turned off. Durr" he answered and Janice screwed her face remembering that she had turned it off after taking Eric's photographs.

"Whoops sorry darling. How long have you been waiting?" she asked throwing him the keys.

"I just walked in a few minutes before you arrived, and believe me you scared the pants off me when I saw three gorgeous but very different women enter my house. Not that you're not all gorgeous..." he spluttered.

"Time to go Tim, we know what you mean and we don't want to be responsible for someone dying because we held you up."

"No of course not, only I had a call from Dennis Fortescue apparently his wife has had a funny turn and needs some sedation. Nothing really wrong with Cecile that a good kick up the backside wouldn't cure, but please don't quote me, confidentiality and all that."

As they heard the car drive away at speed all three collapsed laughing, knowing that Dennis must have waited as long as he dared before resorting to calling the doctor.

It was dark when Jayne opened the kitchen door and saw that the clock in the kitchen read a quarter to six.

The aroma of cooking filled the room, and the table had been set for two, but there was no sign of Rory.

"Be out in a minute, dinner is about done. I hope you don't but I thought you might be hungry, and well I used my initiative?"

"That's lovely and very thoughtful; I'll just go and get changed." She called back to the study door.

She slipped out of the red dress and saw that she still had Janice's underwear on, and she stood admiring herself in the mirror.

"Not bad for a forty plus year old." she admitted turning sideways, and to see if she really did have a bigger bottom than she imagined.

"It looks just fine." she said slapping the cheek with her hand.

"It's ready when you are." Rory called up the stairs.

Jayne quickly slipped her house dress on and fastened the buttons.

"Coming." she called back down the stairs.

"Smells lovely." she said entering the warm kitchen.

"Good old Irish stew with soda bread, warm the cockles of your heart as me mam used to say."

"You did all this yourself, including the soda bread?" Jayne asked. "I am impressed."

"Me mam wasn't always a well woman, and so we all had to muck in, and well she was a good teacher."

Where is your family now? Still in Belfast? Jayne asked.

"Not any more mam passed away ten years ago now, and Jerry my older brother lives in Canada, but he's not a well man either, Agnes the eldest sister left home when I was just a kid and no one has heard from her since. And Dad died two weeks ago that's why I went back to Belfast to bury him; there was no one there except a distant few aunts and uncles we used to see at the funerals. Jerry was too ill to travel. So I said my goodbyes to Dad and to Northern Ireland I won't be going back again."

"I am sorry to hear about your father and your brother." Jayne said.

"Jerry won't be long going himself, according to Kathleen his wife, the chemo is not working, and she reckons he has about six months. I know it's sad he's only forty seven, but at least his kids are grown up, and Jerry and I were never close."

"I know its none of my business, but would you mind if I asked you a personal question?" she said.

"I suppose it depends just how personal you want to be." He laughed. "No not at all ask anything you like, so long as you answer one for me that is when I can think of one. Now that's got you stumped hasn't it?" he smiled again.

Jayne ignored the question and continued. "How is it a good looking man with all your culinary skills, and many others I have no doubt, is not married; or perhaps you are, or even divorced. I haven't really asked the question very well, have I?"

"Well enough. No I am not married, never have been, so no divorce. And the truthful answer is, the right girl has never come along, and as the old saying goes the ones you really fall for, are either already married or gay, or indeed both."

Jayne was completely unable to halt the flow of her blush."

"Sorry I didn't mean to embarrass you." Rory said genuinely concerned.

"No." she smiled "It wasn't anything you said, it just happens sometimes, it a woman thing, hormones." She lied unable to think of anything else.

"Well if that s all it is." He said wondering just what it was he said that prompted the reaction; she was certainly not having hormonal problems.

"You mean to say you never came even close to popping the question." Jayne continued her embarrassment over.

"Well I suppose there were a couple of times, but I was very young the first time and in the army, and well she got lonely when I was away in Iraq, and so that ended quickly.

"And the second one?"

"Ah yes Rula Kovak, she was a Polish girl I met in Thailand, and a very nice girl she was to, but my nightmares scared her off, but that was a long time ago now, and it's rare that my past returns to haunt me. The seminary really helped me come to terms with everything. So you can maybe see why my becoming a clergyman was important to me, I have always been obsessive about paying my debts.

"So it's not really about finding god for you then, rather that you feel you owe the church or maybe you feel you owe god, or have I got it all wrong?"

"What you have got wrong, is your mathematics, you asked for one question, and now I am getting worried just when the thumb screws come out of the drawer." He laughed not wanting to question his own reasoning about god and the church.

"Sorry, I am being nosy, but you are the easiest man to talk to that I have ever met, who doesn't want anything in return."

"So a whisky is off the table then?" Rory laughed.

"No of course not, you fool. You know what I meant."

"Indeed I do, but you can't always blame a man for trying when such a beautiful lady like yourself is in the room."

"You and your Irish charm, I shouldn't but it's nice the way you produce it just at the right time. So let's enjoy Jonas's whisky, but please don't let me get soused again, I would hate to become an alcoholic."

"I have just thought of my question." Rory said collecting the empty bowls.

"Is it a personal one?" Jayne's asked.

"Sort of but not embarrassingly personal, well at least I don't think so." He said. But let me ask, and if you don't want to answer that's fine, I'll drink all the whisky on my own."

"Rory for pity's sake, just ask the question." Jayne laughed.

"Well you look different, not different; different. Just not the way you looked when you went out this morning."

Jayne realized that she still had traces of her make-up on.

"Make up and Janice trimmed my eyebrows."

Rory nodded knowingly. "But I don't see that you really need make-up, but then what do I know about what a woman needs, me being something of a confirmed bachelor, perhaps I should have become a priest."

"One thing you never will be, and that's a saint." Jayne giggled leading the way into the lounge with two glasses in her hand.

Chapter 9

"Janice you still have a deal of explaining to do." Tim called through the locked bathroom door.

"I'll be out in a minute, just let me go to the toilet in peace." Janice answered through the door.

"Would you like a cocktail?" he asked pleasantly, wondering if she would tell him the truth about her and her friends dressing up venture, or was he in for one of her fictitious but often amusing tales.

Somehow he leant towards a partial truth, seeing that the vicar's wife was involved, and the memory of Jayne standing against the wall downstairs earlier looking so stunning in the red dress and with her own auburn hair cascading around her shoulder.

He suddenly forgot all about his promise to Jonas as the swelling in his groin became painful. He unzipped his pants and repositioned his erection into a more comfortable position.

"Tim did you hear me?" Janice called

"No sorry my mind was elsewhere." He answered.

"Between your legs again no doubt, anyway I said that I would have a gimlet."

"Gimlet; ok but remind me what goes into a gimlet?" He asked.

"Gin, lots of it. Lime juice, sugar and a twist of lemon to garnish."

"Yes of course I remember, I think I'll have the same." He said turning to leave.

"Why not make a jug full while you're at it?" she called after him.

"Of course. Ok when you are ready."

She heard him heavy footed down the stairs, and she returned the douche bag to the cupboard and slipped her light housecoat over her still damp naked body, and began to descend the stairs.

Haydn's the miracle symphony was overflowing from the carefully hidden surround sound system in the lounge.

"He is waiting to seduce me." She whispered to herself and she swiftly backtracked up into their bedroom and stripped off her housecoat before walking herself through a mist of Chanel No 5, and stepping into the new black cocktail dress she bought earlier in Salisbury's most expensive boutique. And with the red high heels and the blonde wig Jayne had worn, and a few moments in front of the dressing table mirror she again descended the stairs.

"You took your ti…Wow!" Tim said a little breathlessly, the thought of Jayne evaporating as he turned to greet his different but gorgeous wife with her cocktail in his hand.

"Janice darling you look amazingly different, with that wig on I thought for a moment you had snuck Jayne back into the house, but I am glad that it's you."

"Not sure quite how I should take that." Janice smiled seductively sipping her cocktail. "But it's obvious you would have been happy to see either of us; or by the feel of you." She said stroking his enormous bulge in his trousers. "I guess you could maybe handle us both together."

She giggled as his thick cock twitched and became even firmer.

"My gosh; so you do fancy screwing me and the vicar's wife at the same time." Janice whispered huskily

The thought of seeing Tim's huge prick impaling Janice while Jayne knelt over her face letting her suckle her clitoris as Tim slid in and out of her friends vagina, sent several tremors of excitement shuddering through her body.

"By the reaction of your lovely tits, I can see that the thought of such an event would certainly not go amiss with you either."

Janice's knowing smile added even more hardness to his erection.

"So tell me, we both know that I am the only man in the village who is aware of the aims of Mary's and yours, Widows and Orphans association, but I am having trouble believing that poor naive Jayne the wife of our vicar has been inveigled into your lesbian activities.

Janice's nonchalant smile made Tim's eyes rise.

"How on earth did you manage that?" he added disbelievingly.

"No guilty this time and well Jayne was talking to Mary and asked why she hadn't been asked to any of the meetings. I think she thought as the wife of the vicar she should be involved. Of course she had no idea of what we got up to. Anyway Mary took it upon herself to try and explain to her what it was all about. And from what I gather from Mary, once Jayne had an inkling of what Mary was alluding to, well she sort of took over, and by accident I sort of walked in on them."

"What you mean?" Tim asked creating a picture in his mind that instantly rejuvenated his flagging member.

"No not actually doing anything, so you can control that cock of yours before it pokes you eye out." Janice laughed, as Tim eased his erection up against his stomach.

"And?" Tim asked urging her to continue with her story.

"Well like I said I didn't actually catch them in the sexual act. However I did notice that Jayne was not wearing any pants or brassiere, and in her hast had buttoned her blouse up wrongly."

"So?" Tim asked his hand now stroking his erection through his trousers.

"Well you know me darling, and she does have a great body. So I thought why not it was obvious that Mary had already been involved, and as it turned out she was up for everything; not that we did much; I mean we were in Mary's kitchen, and it was blatantly apparent that she had been starved of love, for well I guess almost all of her married life, and thinking about the way she looks and looking at Jonas, I can only surmise that Jonas caught her on the rebound from a failed relationship; and as a recently appointed clergyman saw her as an asset to obtaining a parish of his own, plus the fact that she was what we now call 'arm candy' and you have to admit she does look the part."

"Indeed she does." Tim agreed his eyes glazing a little at the thought of Jayne naked with her legs apart.

The CD finished and seconds later Tchaikovsky's first symphony began.

"Another drink?" Tim asked downing the rest of his in one large swallow.

"Please darling." Janice answered crossing her legs and allowing her dress to ride up revealing the tops of her shapely thighs.

"Another Gimlet or a bloody Mary?" Tim asked his hand trembling slightly.

"Bloody Mary." Janice answered after a few moments comparing the choices.

"I'll stick with the Gimlet." Tim said pouring Janice's Vodka and tomato juice cocktail first.

"Right so you have filled in some of the background, and I have to agree that I have been totally astounded by your revelations, but then nearly all your revelations constantly amaze me, which is just one of the reasons I am so totally in love with you. But you still have to explain the façade this afternoon. You did truly frighten the pants of me when the three of you just walked into the house."

"What like the witches of Eastwick?" Janice giggled

"Precisely; but I know that was never part of the plan, but now I suppose you had better explain. And if you don't mind Janice can we stick to the truth, I know just how far you take your fantasies sometimes and as brilliant as they are…"

"Alright Tim, the truth and as much of the truth as I can; I mean we both a confidentiality issues; agreed." Janice said seriously.

"Agreed." Tim replied settling himself opposite her and sliding down into the comfortable chair his eyes focusing on what was just beyond his view.

He knew from past experience if Janice's story became awkward for her, then as was her usual ploy, she would open her legs to distract him, and Tim didn't want to miss the event.

Janice explained about the sex shop and the plan to buy some things to enhance the Widows and Orphans activities.

Tim hid his smile behind his Gimlet but said nothing.

She explained both Jayne's and Mary's concern about being recognized, and she agreed that perhaps they should go incognito."

"Well my dear you certainly managed that." Tim interrupted.

"Yes it was just as well we did, as it turned out it seemed as if the whole village had decided to make the journey to Salisbury. First of all we bumped into Tom Browner's son Terrence and he never recognized any of us. So we went shopping I bought this and a number of other things."

Tim's face fell as he dreaded to credit card bill.

"And Jayne well she bought underwear that will give Jonas apoplexy if he ever sees her wearing it."

Again Tim felt a twitching in his groin.

But then as it was getting late we decided it was time to visit the sex shop, and that was when we were accosted by none other than the snooty Cicely Fortescue, and Dennis, who really deserves someone less of a bully than his wife.

Tim's ears pricked up at hearing the councilor's wife's name.

"So what happened between you and Cicely?" Tim asked nervously.

Janice explained that Cicely had made a loud comment about Jayne wearing a real fur coat.

"Jayne looked on the verge of tears as she was about to humiliate Jayne, so I grabbed the old cow and in my best east End accent I told her I would kick her cunt up into her mouth if she didn't apologize, and a few other things. Well she apologized and we left, but Tim you have to believe me Dennis loved it."

"Is that all?" Tim asked remembering Cicely's version as being completely different, and recalling Dennis's eyes focused on the ceiling and his head shaking from side to side.

"Yes I think…Oh no, you will never guess who we saw in the sex shop ogling through the gay men magazines. Hang on a moment." She said reaching for her mobile phone, and flipping through the several aps.

"Ah here they are." She cried discovering the three photographs she had taken inside the shop.

She handed the phone across to Tim.

"Oh my god." Tim said slowly letting each word make its own statement.

"I knew there was something a little strange about our postman, but I never dreamt that he leant that way, but come to think of it, a lot of his emotional complaints do actually fit into this ort of pattern. But Janice you can't allow these pictures to be seen. I mean not only will it destroy the poor man, think of his wife and daughters."

"Tim how could you ever think I would do that, but the sneaky little bastard snooping and his constant innuendoes in the pub will end believe me, only Eric himself will see them, then even though he won't know. I will delete them."

Tim laughed "Janice I only hope I never get on the wrong side of you?"

"Either side of me is great with you darling, now please another drink. And well you know the rest of the story."

Tim refilled Janice's glass as the London Philharmonic selective works of Beethoven CD began to play.

Tim dimmed the lights and sat beside her on the long sofa.

"Would you like me to remove the wig or shall I keep it on and you can pretend that is Jayne you are fucking." Janice laughed kissing him lightly on the lips.

"Keep it on if you like then maybe it will seem like I am fucking the pair of you at the same time." Tim suggested seductively.

"Mmm that sounds nice and interesting, but how do I get my extra fun playing two rolls, how could you feel about the real thing, I mean you me and another lady, maybe Jayne but not necessarily that is if she's agreeable, but I make no promises, but for arguments sake lets just go with you me and another lady of both our approvals of course." Janice asked her hand pressing on his hard erection.

"That's of course if you are up to it." She laughed digging her nails into his sensitive knob through his trousers.

"Of course I am up for it, if you are, I mean I have always loved the thought of you making love to her women, and to tell the truth I have often wanted to be the proverbial fly on the wall, but have respected your privacy on it, but now you say you would like to form a threesome where I can watch and take part. That Janice has to be a yes, yes, yes. But who else do you have in mind?" Tim asked hoping that the obvious choice of Mary would be her answer, he had sampled her charms in a moment of weakness after Teddy died, and because she was a patient he had avoided the temptation ever since, but the memory had continued to resurrect itself from time to time.

"Well I have seen the way you look at Mary sometimes, and don't even deny that you would love to fuck her silly." Janice laughed allowing her legs to open as wide as her new dress would allow.

"Janice please let me take your dress off I want to look at you naked, even after all our time together I never tire of seeing you naked."

Janice smiled and stood up and easing the dress off her shoulders letting it slid to her ankles. She stepped out of it and bent over with parted legs enabling Tim to gaze at her buttocks and vagina.

She folded the dress and laid it over the back of the chair before turning to the still seated Tim. She placed her hands behind his head and pulled him onto her trimmed Veneris Mons with its musky fragrance of her aroused cunt.

She heard his moan of pleasure as he drew her pheromones deep into his lungs, and his tongue licked greedily between her legs.

With her legs astride his knees she pushed her bottom forward making it possible for him to locate her anxiously awaiting clitoris.

"Change places." She urged pulling away from him and sitting on the edge of the sofa while Tim struggled with the belt of his trousers. He dragged them off and kicked them across the room along with his shoes. His silk shirt followed seconds later.

"Socks?" Janice said raising her legs so that Tim had an uninterrupted view of her open vagina.

Tim hurriedly dragged of his offending socks and hurled them after his already abandoned clothes.

"Now it's all yours." Janice said reaching for his head.

Tim's multitalented tongue quickly had Janice moaning in the throes of ecstasy as he brushed and suckled on her labia lips and swollen clitoris until he felt she was on the verge of coming, then he relaxed his efforts and caressed her arsehole the tip of his tongue attempting to force an entry while Janice writhed on the verge of her orgasm.

"Let me fuck you." Janice urged. "Lie on your back I want to ride you cock."

Tim reluctantly pulled his face away from between her legs and lay on his back on the thick carpet.

Janice straddled him with his knob resting between her hanging labia while Tim held a breast in each hand tugging gently on her swollen nipples.

Janice slowly lowered herself down the long shaft clenching and unclenching her muscles as it sank deeper and deeper into her body.

She felt his cock jerking with each of her muscle spasms finally they both gasped as her spread buttock cheeks settled on his pubic bone.

"More darling more." Tim begged as he felt the tips of her fingers grip his own small nipples. He bucked as the searing yet widely erotic pain made is already swollen penis swell even further.

"Janice please ride me now I need to come." Tim begged.

Janice removed her right hand from his nipple and pushed it down behind her until she located his hard testis and her finger slid beneath them until she found the spot she was looking for.

With her finger masturbating his erotic prostrate gland whilst squeezing his sensitive cock with her vagina's muscles combined with the additional pleasure pain of his pinched nipple Tim's balls exploded deep inside her, jerking   several times before his sacks were empty.

Tim flopped back his arms outstretched as he waiting for his body to recover.

"Still fancy that threesome?" Janice whispered squeezing his flaccid cock with her vagina muscles.

"Not right now, but soon, that is if you really are serious." Tim said feeling his cock already reacting.

"I see the thought is having an effect already. Janice said slowly raising herself up off Tim's half hard cock.

"It's your turn now." Tim said as Janice sat back on the edge of the sofa and helped pull him to his feet.

"Stay like that, only lean back the way you were earlier." Tim said dropping to his knees.

Janice hooked her knees behind her forearms and pulled herself wide open.

Shuddering as a trickle of Tim's semen ran down over her sensitive arsehole.

Tim's tongue caught it before it dripped onto the cream coloured sofa.

"Mmm that feels nice." Janice whispered as she felt Tim's tongue lick more of the creamy spunk as it dribbled from inside her lovingly abused vagina.

Tim's mouth covered her aroused hole while his tongue brushed across her fully emerged clitoris.

"Tim, please don't stop this time all the way. Oh my god yes!" Janice screamed as she felt herself coming.

As her orgasm peaked the remainder of Tim's spunk shot from her pulsating vagina expelling the remainder of his semen from her and into his mouth dribbling down his chin.

"Don't swallow." Janice gasped as she dropped her legs and dragged Tim's face up to her own.

Her tongue licked around his mouth before she forced her tongue into his spunk filled mouth.

Drained they sat back in the sofa bathed in each others perspiration and finishing off their cocktails.
Her head lay on his chest and his arm draped round her shoulders.
"You know darling that sometimes all this feels too good to be true, and occasionally it frightens me that it might all end one day."
"Well until we are both ninety-six and die after a night such as this let's get as much from life that we want." He laughed squeezing her tighter to him.
"I really do love you Doctor." She giggled.
"What's funny?" he asked.
"Oh I was just thinking if you could write prescriptions for evenings like this, you could cure the world of all its ailments, medical and political."
"Of course but that's the job for the guy upstairs."
"What man upstairs...Oh you mean God? I thought for a mad second that you might have organized another threesome the other way round, and I have to say that, that doesn't really appeal to me." She giggled.
"Me neither, but your version is really beginning to work." Tim said.
"So I see you Tim are insatiable at time, are you on a Viagra drip at work." She asked.
"Now that is something I hadn't thought of but perhaps a couple of tablets, if I have two beautiful women to satisfy. Now I don't know about you but I have surgery tomorrow and after you almost hospitalized Mrs. Fortescue, I think your dressing up days in Salisbury should become just a memory, and so I am off for my beauty sleep before you find another way of arousing the hungry beast." He

laughed and stood up and waggled his already swelling penis at her.

Chapter 10

Rory was clearing away the breakfast plates when Janice burst into the kitchen.

"Jayne I have…" She stopped mid sentence as she noticed Rory at the kitchen sink.

"Oh hello you must be…Rory, of course, Jayne did mention something about a temporary replacement for Jonas, not that I attend church that often, but I might well see if I can revive my interest. Sorry Jayne but he is a definite improvement of your husband, and it appears that he is house trained as well. Perhaps a word in the bishop's ear and you could do a straight swap."

"Janice!" Jayne said loudly, while Rory burst out laughing.

"You my dear lady, can only be the doctor's wife, Janice I believe?"

"Right first time, so what has Jayne been saying about me that you recognize me so easily?"

"Only that you were an extremely attractive and sophisticated lady, who she is extremely fond of."

Rory said smiling and gazing into her eyes.

Janice felt her legs wobble momentarily as she forced herself to look away.

"He is also extremely diplomatic, oh just wait till the rest of the village women clasp their eyes on him, there will be more converts than St Peter made himself."

"That is rather stretching things a little far and anyway in a little under six weeks and I shall be gone, back into the world. And your regular vicar will be back."

"You make that sound more like a curse than something we should look forward to." Janice said dragging a chair out and pouring herself a cup of coffee.

"I gather you are not altogether happy with the Reverend Beech?" Rory asked.

"Oh you mean Jonas, well no not really, but then I have little to do with him. Tim that's my husband is friendly with him, but he certainly isn't someone I would want to have any form of discussion with. Sorry Jayne I know he's your husband and all that."

"No that's fine, I can see how you and Jonas would clash, and I much prefer not to have Jonas upset. He can get quite tiresome. Well now you have managed to introduce yourselves, what was it you called round for, other than to meet the new vicar of course?" Jayne asked.

"No to be honest I had completely forgotten about Jonas's replacement." Janice lied beautifully, avoiding Rory's searching eyes.

"Just a chat really but perhaps we can meet over at the Grange later?"

"Sorry ladies, if you want to talk I have this wedding to sort out, and I suppose I should introduce myself to Mary, who I gather does all the church flowers perhaps I too could pop over and visit later at the Grange?

"Down the lane turn right and the large open gates will take you to Mary's if no one answers just walk round the back you'll probably find her in the conservatory. It's just an enormous greenhouse really, but give her a shout first we don't want her jumping out of her knickers do we?" Janice giggled.

"No of course not." He said almost smiling at the image his mind created.

"Anyway Jayne come on I can tell you and Mary my news, and we can also tell Mary to expect a tall dark handsome stranger who looks absolutely nothing like a clergyman. Rory before you disappear, do you have a dog collar at all?"

"Indeed I do but only for religious events. I feel it tends to restrict conversation." He replied.

"Well that bits true enough." Janice said recalling the few men of god she had come into contact with.

They found Mary in the kitchen with her Mrs. Beeton cookery book open.

"What's for lunch then?" Janice asked striding in and pouring coffee into the three waiting china mugs.

"I don't know I was just trying to decide, its terribly difficult cooking for one."

"Well that's where we can help." Janice said just to stop the confusion we will stay for lunch, and as a bonus the vicar has invited himself over as well."

"No he hasn't." Jayne said

"All he said was that he felt he should introduce himself, as you were doing the flowers for Saturday."

"I just hope he is not going to poke his nose in telling what he wants, or anything like that; I mean your Jonas tried it once but I soon put him in his place?" Mary protested.

Jayne laughed "No Mary he is nothing at all like that, he and Jonas are worlds apart, in fact I hardly believe that he is a vicar at all."

"That's true." Janice added "He looks more like an American lumberjack, Check shirt and jeans, and a face that wouldn't look out of place on a calendar. I am surprised Jayne has managed to keep her hands off him."

"Janice! Goodness me the man has only just arrived, and he is a clergyman, and I am a married woman; what on earth would he want with the likes of me. He is just a very nice good man, who has had some problems in his life before he found god." Jayne said angrily.

"Whoops sorry, I was only kidding, but he does look at you in a funny but nice sort of way. But it appears that you have learnt quite a bit about reverend…?"

"Killeen. Well yes we have talked and he is very easy to talk to, but to be honest we had both drunk rather more of Jonas's single malt that we intended, and we both probably said more about our lives than we intended, so I would rather not reveal things that he might not approve of." Jayne said.

"Quite right." Mary said. "If he wants us to know about his past, I am sure he will tell us in his own good time. And you say you have invited him to lunch?"

"No we didn't invite him; all he said was that he would come over and introduce himself later." Janice smiled.

"Well then I had better make myself presentable." Mary said smiling.

"You think I should wear underclothes for the occasion or just the see through dress." She giggled.

"Mary you really are incorrigible." Janice said grinning.

"After yesterday when you threatened to kick poor old Cicely's cunt up to her mouth, and got away with it, nothing I could ever do could come close to being incorrigible." Mary laughed at the memory.

"Just stay as you are Mary you look fine." Jayne said.

"But should I at least put some drawers on?"

"Only if you are going to lift you skirt above your head." Janice said shaking her head.

"So what do you fancy for lunch remembering that I am knickerless?"

"Food Mary as lovely as it is we still need food to sustain us. Now what's have you in the fridge?" Jayne asked.

"Its quicker to ask what isn't in the fridge." Janice said pulling the huge double doored fridge open.

"I see what you mean." Jayne said.

"I was thinking of lobster chowder. My monthly fish man delivered early this morning and I had three fresh lobsters."

That sounds delicious do you want us to help?" Janice asked the note of reluctance easily visible in her voice."

"Well I am not too keen of dropping the poor things into boiling water, but after that I am fine.

"Oh that's the easy bit; so long as they have been in the fridge they are comatose anyway. So put the pan on and I'll murder your lobsters for you." Janice laughed.

"Now Mary I have news and I was rather hoping that you could come to the rescue."

"If I can, then you know I will." Mary replied.

"If you remember the game we played and…."

"Yes." Jayne and Mary chorused.

"Well I have found just the man who is willing to take part in what he thinks is a threesome but I know we can easily persuade him into a foursome. I know if I had said that he would have to satisfy three women he would have refused, but he trusts me to deliver"

"Who on earth do you know that would agree to that and how do you know if we might want to go with him. Janice that game was just a bit of fantasy not meant to be taken literally." Mary said shocked that her friend had taken it beyond what it was supposed to be.

"Just wait till you hear who it is then tell me it won't work." Janice begged.

"Ok who is the lothario, and please don't say Charles Dunning because I may just do to you what you threatened Cicely with." Mary giggled insanely for several minutes.

Janice waited until she had calmed down,

"No it certainly isn't Charles believe it or not it's Tim."

"What your husband Tim?" Mary asked disbelievingly. "Now I know you are winding us up"

"No its perfectly true, after yesterday, and well Tim misses nothing and you also know that what Tim is aware of, remains with Tim, its more than his jobs worth to suffer loose lips, well anyway last night I dressed up in the blonde wig and to cut a long story short after I asked a number of leading questions I learnt that not only was he keen but ecstatic at the thought, he kept asking if I minded and of course I told him that it was absolutely fine with me and I wanted it as much as he obviously did."

But Tim?" Jayne said wanting desperately to fulfill her fantasy but afraid to commit to it.

She was fine with Mary and Janice as that was something she had yearned for since Theresa had died, but suddenly the thought of Janice's husband her own husband's friend".

"Come on say yes, its just once and your fantasy is fulfilled."

"I only wrote that I wanted to watch." Jayne protested.

"Yes but when I asked if you would like to take part, you never actually said no." Janice argued.

"Well I suppose not but that was before your husband was involved."

"So who else is there that comes even close to being acceptable. And I gather the new vicar is off the table?"

Jayne suddenly erupted into a fit of uncontrollable laughter.

"Janice Harding you have to one of the nicest and most terrible person I have ever met. Ok but I reserve the right to chicken out, I mean you say he is expecting a threesome well there's you and Mary that's the three. How would he feel about screwing the lady of the manor so to speak?"

"Happy as a pig in the proverbial, and I know Mary would just love to get her hands on Tim's monumental prick wouldn't you."

Mary blushed. "Have I been that obvious" she asked smiling.

"Mary you are at the top of a long list of his patients who have heard of it size and would love to have an opportunity to use it. But Tim is probably the most professional man around. Oh don't get me wrong the man is certainly no saint but his discretion goes far beyond the norm. So it's a date then Janice said grinning like a Cheshire cat

"Now Mary the balls in your court." Janice concluded.

"Fear not girls I have the perfect place, and please Janice I don't want you getting angry that you haven't been privy to it before. I have been saving it for a special occasion, and well this is about as special as you can get."

"What place and where is it? You crafty woman." Janice asked wondering where it could be.

She had been round the Grange many times and its multiple bedrooms were just that, bedrooms.

Then she recalled the locked door on the landing that Mary insisted led to the storage space in the attic.

So where ever Mary had planned for the forthcoming event it most certainly had to be up there.

"Are you going to reveal your secret then?" Janice asked.

"Later be patient, all will be revealed in good time>" Mary grinned lasciviously.

Between them they broke open the lobsters and retrieved the succulent meat, and chopped the onions and celery, while Mary peeled the potatoes and diced the peppers.

Two cartons of fresh double cream went into the pot, and they left it simmering, while Janice struggled to get Mary to tell more about the place she was so secretive about.

"Ready." Mary said stopping the timer before it rang.

"Mary there's enough her to feed an army." Janice said turning the cookery book round." To feed six it says here." She said

"Looks like its Lobster chowder all week then." Jayne chuckled.

A sudden rapping on the front door made them all jump.

"Sounds like your door bell is broken." Janice said just as the jangling of the bell echoed into the kitchen

"That probably Rory." Jayne said getting up from the table.

"Nose like a bloodhound if he smelt the lobster from the vicarage." Janice giggled.

"Who's going to answer the door?" Jayne asked do you want me to."

"No dear he might think you are the maid and thinks he can take advantage of you." She laughed.

Mary glanced in the entrance hall mirror and patted her hair into place.

She swung the door open to the tall dark handsome vicar's wide smile.

"Good afternoon I presume you are Rory our new vicar, and very nice too, please come in and I hope you like lobster chowder, because I have apparently made enough for six and we are only three, well four now you are here. So now that the niceties are completed, come and help us remedy my cooking error.

"Mary you are a darling, I love lobster chowder and I haven't had it since I left Thailand years ago. So lead the way I am assuming my landlady and the doctor's wife are you're two other guests." Rory said finally peeling Mary's hand from his own.

"Perceptive as well as handsome; young man you will go far in this life, but I have no idea just how far any of will go in the life hereafter."

"Ladies I believe you know our guest who has promised to help with lunch.

"Hello Jayne, Mrs. Harding." Rory said cheerfully drawing up a chair.

"Janice, Please or I shall be forced to call you Reverend Kolling; sorry Killeen slip of the tongue.

We were discussing a book Jayne had come across written by a Rik Kolling, a couple of days ago, and the name has sort of stuck in my head, and I have tried numerous engine searches and can't seem to find any reference to him. But it certainly wouldn't be a book you have come across in your line of work.

"Are you alright Revere…Rory?" Mary asked "You have gone very pale, would you like some water?"

"No Mary I'm fine, I occasionally get a funny turn, something to do with my time abroad. No I shall be fine in a moment." Rory's mind wondering if indeed it Janice had made an unintentional slip, or were they aware of his past.

"Jayne had felt herself redden but thankfully no one noticed that she saw but she had deliberately avoided looking in Rory's direction.

"You're right and yes I would probably remember a name like that, and no sorry I can't help you but I shall be honoured to call you Janice, It's a lovely name and well I am not what you call a formal sort of person."

The moment passed although Jayne also wondered why Janice had mixed up the names, it was if she had some sort of instinct, But she dismissed the idea just Janice being Janice.

"This chowder is delicious, cream instead of evaporated milk, the difference is amazing, and would it be cheeky to ask for seconds?" Rory asked the colour already returned to his face.

Jayne dared a quick glance and was relieved to see that Rory was smiling at her.

"It's easy to see that you two are getting on well." Mary said."

"Yes well we did turn out to be very different people to what we were expecting."

Mary and Janice burst out laughing, well I suppose we did go a little extreme." Janice said.

"As did I." Rory admitted "But this does seem to be an idyllic place to live." He added.

"So long as you don't scratch the surface too deeply." Mary said.

"Small communities always seem to have many more secrets than you can imagine, but on the hole yes it is a nice place to live if one has a few good friends, otherwise it can be lonelier that the city of London, or the middle of a desert." Mary said wistfully recalling the dark days after Teddy died.

"Would you like to finish it off?" Mary asked filling his bowl before he had a chance to answer.

"That'll put lead into your pencil." She said without thinking.

Both Janice and Jayne gasped and struggled to contain themselves.

"What's the matter with you pair I only said…Oh my god did I really say that to the vicar. I am so sorry."

Rory too almost choked on his chowder but saw the funny side on Mary off the cuff comment, as all four roared with laughter.

In between her bubbling fits Mary kept apologizing and causing even more laughter.

After Rory had said his goodbyes and returned to complete the sermon he had planned for the coming Sunday, they retired to the lounge.

"Well thank the lord he has a sense of humour." Mary said "I really had no idea what I had said; I know I wouldn't have said anything like that if he had been wearing his dog collar. I just hope he doesn't use it somehow in his sermon. He looks the sort that just might." Mary chuckled. "He really is a lovely man though; it's a shame your husband has to come back.

Not that I have anything against him, but he's not a patch on this new one."

"I know it's an awful thing to say and I wouldn't say it anyone except the both of you, but I am rather dreading the thought of Jonas coming back." Jayne admitted.

"Enough about vicars and gloom and doom; and returning to the fun side of life I was thinking of striking while the iron was hot, just in case Tim starts to get cold feet but I am sure I can bring him round again although I am not sure how long it might take. So what about tomorrow night, are you up for it?"

Tomorrow?" Jayne paled even whiter that Rory had earlier.

"I don't think, No Janice I know you have done a lot for me, but honestly I really don't feel I can go through with it. If I could be a fly on the wall I would dearly love to be able to watch, but I mean its early days for me, and so much has happened in such a short time and well, No I am sorry I just can't go through with it."

Janice saw that Jayne was getting stressed beyond what she might have expected.

"Fine Jayne please don't get yourself all wound up, we do what we do because we want to, and we want to do what makes us feel good. And I am sure we can sort something out, can't we Mary?"

Mary's smiled knowingly. "Wait till you see what we have Jayne. Believe me I know this will work out fine for us all. So forget about being involved. I promise you that you will be ably to lie back and enjoy the show without anyone knowing you are there, except Janice and me that is, and we will make sure you don't miss a thing and knowing you are watching makes it even more exciting for us both."

"Well can we at least think about it for a few days" Jayne asked. I mean it doesn't have to be right away. I mean let me at least get used to the idea.

"Well alright I am sure Tim will wait, it will make him all the more receptive anyway, and it's just me that's impatient." Janice said.

Chapter 11

What do you for fun around here other than the pub, and the conversation seems to go very quiet each time I walk into the bar. It's as if Jesus himself had entered and was expecting everyone to buy him a beer. I have tried different cologne's but nothing seems to help." Rory asked sipping another whisky.

"Putting yourself up a bit on the scale Jesus himself." Jayne said reverently, and hiding her smile.

"You know what I mean perhaps that wasn't the best of analogies. But I am beginning to fee like some sort of pariah."

"It could be because everyone knows you are the vicar and a newby to boot, never a god conversational mix and well Jonah was hardly the pub sort so they probably feel uneasy and not quite sure where you are coming from. But what about Reg I heard you and he were buddies in the day." Jayne asked.

"Well we knew about each other, rather than boozing pals, and conversation revolves around. Remember this guy or that guy who died who got wounded and who survived a part of my life I have been trying to forget and even that seemed to have exhausted our conversations."

"Well that's village life which is why most of the youngsters decamp for the bright lights as soon as they are old enough" Jayne commiserated with him.

"How would you like to go to the cinema with me, it's never much fun on your own, and there is an old movie I would rather like to see at the Globe in Devises?" Rory asked putting the newspaper down.

"You mean go to the cinema together what ever would people say?" Jayne giggled.

"Yes I see what you mean people are so narrow minded. I mean it's not as if it was a date or anything." Rory said apologetically

"No of course not and Rory I would love to go to the cinema with you it's been years since I last went, and we could go for a meal afterwards, Dutch of course. Do you think I should get Janice to make me up again just in case we bump into anyone we know?" Jayne grin belied her meaning.

"Now you are being ridiculous, besides I prefer you the way you are, and you were just winding me up right?"

"Yes sorry, and what difference does it make if anyone does see us, its not as if we are doing anything wrong is it?" Jayne said wishing the opposite were true.

"Indeed we are not, well the first showing starts at six, but usually there is half an hour of adverts. So if we leave here at about a quarter to six, we should get there in plenty of time." Rory said. "So that's a date then for tomorrow evening."

"Of course it is, so long as you buy me a bag of popcorn." She laughed.

The next day dragged as Janice was busy completing Tim's tax return that should have been done months earlier and Mary had some workmen in and was fussing around them.

Jayne caught up on what washing she that had built up, and her housework, with her eyes continually watching the clock all day. She chided herself several times for being foolish.

"They were going to the cinema and for a meal as friends she kept telling herself and yet nothing seemed to dampen her excitement.

Rory had been called out, a dying farmer's wife needed someone to talk to and her husband and two sons were too busy with the farm.

Rory had unearthed an old bicycle from the shed and had spent a day restoring it to roadworthiness, and it got him around the parish and kept him fit he said.

At five o clock Jayne was still on edge so she showered and changed into her new underwear, not that Rory would see it but it made her feel young again. She wore a below the knee length dress and the new leather boots the other purchase was a long fitted grey coat that she would put on when they were leaving.

With time to waste while she waited for Rory's return she retrieved the book from under the mattress and continued to read it, she had six more chapters left and each time she opened it and began to read she quickly became absorbed into the story. And soon her breathing became laboured as she felt her body responding to his words. He certainly knew what made women tick and yearn for more than their usual boring lives. He made them come alive and feel wonderful about what life might be like.

The sudden sound of the door opening made her jumps and she hastily shoved the book back out of sight.

"Want a drink before we leave?" Jayne asked entering the kitchen.

"Good idea at least I am done with the bike today so drink driving is not an issue."

Just have a quick shower and get changed gives us about fifteen minutes then before Reg arrives.

Jayne had drunk her whisky before Rory appeared dress in casual trousers white shirt and a black leather jacket.

Just as Reg pulled onto the drive Rory heard the car and downed his drink in three large swallows.

"Reg is a little early." He said holding Jayne's coat for her.

"No comments mate, we are off to the cinema and a meal, this lady never gets out, so let's not make it the talk of the village, you know better than I do what gossips can do."

"Right you are Rory, mums the word, what you off to see?" He asked.

"Something about a nightmare on some street." Jayne said.

"Nightmare on Elm Street; I hope you like being scared then." He laughed.

"Is it very frightening?" she asked Rory.

"No it's just a movie, and I always seemed to miss it, it's very predictable and funny really, so long as you don't take it seriously." He saw Reg raise his eyebrows in the rear view mirror.

The cinema was practically empty except for a pair of in-love teenagers in the back row and an elderly couple who sat right at the front.

Even as the film started Jayne jumped and grabbed Rory's hand and buried her face into his shoulder and after it had ended she was still gripping his hand.

"That was about the most frightening film I have ever seen." she said. "But it was fun." she added as they walked down the high street and realizing they were still holding hands she glanced around and with her free hand she pulled up the high collar of her new coat round the side of her face.

"Where are you taking me to eat?" she asked knowing that Rory was holding onto her hand as much as she was holding his.

"Thai curry house just a few minutes walk, they serve the best Thai curry outside of Bangkok." Rory whispered "And we are here just down this street."

The small tiny restaurant was almost full, but Rory was ushered to the small reserved table in a small alcove at the rear of the eating area.

"I've never eaten Thai curry before." Jayne whispered allowing Rory to help her off with her coat.

"Leave it to me and you will love the flavours." Rory said calling the waiter over and rattling of what appeared to Jayne as a garbled list.

The waiter beamed to hear his own language being spoken, and within minutes the first of several dishes appeared from behind the coloured strips of plastic that hid the small kitchen from the eating area.

Rory explained what was in each dish and Jayne ate everything to the delight of the small waiter.

"That was extraordinarily delicious." She said sipping her glass of potent Thai rice wine.

"And now it is time Cinderella was home before the witching hour." Rory laughed holding her coat and paying the waiter behind her back.

Reg was waiting for them in the town square.

"Enjoy the film?" he asked laughing as Jayne pulled a face.

"It was rather scary but unrealistic, and it certainly made a nice change." She answered.

"Somehow I can't see your old man taking you to the cinema." Reg said.

"No it's certainly not Jonas's thing at all." Jayne agreed.

Jayne hadn't noticed until she was about to get out of the taxi that she had again taken hold of Rory's hand and she quickly pulled it away as Reg opened the door.

"Entering the kitchen Jayne suddenly turned and felt an overwhelming urge to kiss Rory, for what seemed like an age they looked into each others eyes before Rory forced himself the break the impasse.

Jayne knew she had been close to stepping over the mark, and in an attempt to break the two second silence that seemed like hours she suddenly laughed.

"We were supposed to be going Dutch so what do I owe you?" She asked still wanting to throw her arms around him.

"You can pay next week." Rory laughed.

"So we are off out again next week, any why not, by the way that rice wine was pretty potent stuff." She said forcing herself to look away from him.

The following week Tim was called away to Spain where his mother and father had bought a small apartment in Marbella in Spain where they had taken to spending the best part of the year.

Marie his mother had been taken ill, and insisted that her doctor son was the only person capable of treating her.

So with a locum installed in the practice Tim spent the next two weeks in Marbella looking after what he reckoned was an extreme bout of hypochondria and wanted her son around.

Meanwhile Janice and friends enjoyed their new found liberty.

Not that Tim ever put any restrictions on Janice whatsoever, but she said it was good occasionally to spend a little time apart it revitalized the relationship.

The following week Rory and Jane visited the same almost deserted cinema and watched another horror film, which gave Jayne the opportunity to hold onto Rory's hand and they dined again at the same restaurant, who welcomed them like long lost relatives and again Rory settled the bill before Jayne had a chance to get to her purse.

"Ah well." Rory said. "There is always the next time."

Other evenings they sat and talked about everything and nothing both feeling completely at ease with each other.

Secretly Rory continued with his novel about Jayne and himself, allowing his fantasies to flourish far beyond what he deemed ever being possible.

Jonas hadn't telephoned or written Jayne assumed that he was busy with the bishop and became something from the distant past, and Jayne continued to meet up with Janice and Mary but some of the early fire had waned a little but they all three seemed satisfied with their loving and companionship.

Tim's telephone message to say that he was returning home the following day meant that Janice picked him up at six in the morning at Heathrow and they stopped off in a discreet lay by to take the edge of their lust.

Chapter 13

"What do you mean you would rather not? I thought you were all for it three weeks ago?" Janice said angrily.

"I was then, but I wasn't really serious, and after what you said about Jayne being willing, the idea sounded fantastic I mean she has a great body and she didn't look like Jonas's wife, but since then I have given it some thought over the past couple of weeks, and you have to agree she's the bloody wife of our vicar and a patient. I could get struck off if it ever came out, and don't tell me this won't come out. No I am sorry but the risk is too great."

"So Dr Harding you are telling me that you haven't screwed a patient before." Janice said smugly. "Because I know at least three of your patients who have had your dick inside them, and it's no good denying it. So what's the real reason, and it's certainly not because you are shy either. So that just leaves the fact that she is the vicar's wife, and since when have you ever been smitten by religion?"

"Yes alright it is to do with Jonas. Before he left he made me promise that I would keep an eye on Jayne while he was away. I think he was worried about her being on her own with the deputy vicar. He wasn't specific but he well sort of hinted' anyway I agreed, and I know I have been somewhat derelict in doing just that, because I wasn't keen on the idea anyway, but that way I could honestly say that I saw nothing out of the ordinary, unless you call dressing up, as being out of the ordinary, but then that woman looked nothing like Jayne anyway, and when she's with you girls doing what you do, its not quite the same as fucking her myself, and Jonas is not an easy man to lie to. So there it is."

"But you screwed Mary just a few months after Ted died and that never bothered you, nor did it bother me, not that you were aware I knew and Mary has never mentioned it either; but you and Mary are pretty transparent, and well Mary is special and we both know that we have a wonderful arrangement when it comes to sex."

Tim guilty smile wasn't lost on his wife.

"So if we remove Jayne from the equation will it bother you if I were to ask you to have a threesome with Mary and me then?"

Tim's eyes lit up and a sly grin took the serious look from his face

"Not at all, but does Mary know what you are planning; I wouldn't want to surprise her, and please try to explain to Jayne that it's not her. I would dearly have loved to have experienced the three of us, but I am certain she will understand, I mean she knows Jonas better than anyone."

"Ok darling, I do understand and I am certain that Jayne will as well, and to be honest I rather think she was trying to get out of the situation anyway." Janice smiled deviously

"And you put me through all that, knowing how she felt. I'm beginning to think it was you who wanted to watch me screw her."

"Well it would have been nice." Janice laughed. "So Mr. Horny are you busy this evening?"

"Free as a bird after I have checked in with the locum Doctor Morris today and then I can do evening surgery after that well I have a lot of catching up to do." Tim replied leeringly.

"Good because Mary is as keen as mustard, so I can only assume that you must have performed well previously."

Tim smiled innocently. "Right that's a date seven-thirty at the Grange, and I am really looking forward to it.

"Evidently by the swelling in your lower regions." Janice replied staring at the bulge in his trousers "Apparently we have the use of a sauna and jacuzzi so be prepared, other than that I am afraid until later this afternoon I am about as in the dark as you are. Mary has been most secretive, and she has told me a little about her and Teddy's special room in the old servant's quarters, and she has had several men in working up there but has categorically refused to allow me up there or to answer any questions."

The knowing look on Tim's face brought a frown to her own, as if Tim knew something she didn't.

"Sounds bloody good to me." Tim said feeling his prick harden at the thought of his wife and the more voluptuous Mary performing together and with him screwing them both.

Like many men, Tim often fancied having sex with the older and softer women, almost as much as he did with his slender well breasted wife sex driven wife.

"Right now that's sorted I must away to afternoon surgery. I will probably shower at work, and I will see you both at the Grange; I haven't seen Teddy's romper room since he died."

"I wasn't aware you knew about it?" Janice said curiously knowing full well that Mary had never mentioned Tim in relation to her secret room, let alone knowing its name.

"I only went up there once very briefly; Teddy telephoned and said he was having trouble with the stairs, and Mary was out, so I just got a quick glimpse, and he made me swear not to tell Mary that I had been up into their private den; and so you have to keep that secret as well."

He kissed her briefly on the cheek, and squeezed her bottom before dashing out to his car.

"See you this evening then." She called just before she heard the car door slam.

"Right Jayne I have managed to get you off the hook, but it took a bit of doing, but Tim is a practical sort of man. And would you believe that your darling Jonas made Tim promise to keep an eye on you while he was away. Apparently Tim got the impression Jonas was worried about you being alone in the vicarage with his temporary replacement. Well he put Tim in a position that he could hardly refuse. Not that he has taken any such steps to keep an eye on you that is; but he doesn't feel happy about screwing his friend's wife, especially after promising to keep an eye on her. Plus the fact that he rather thinks that Jonas would see through him if he fucked you into the bargain and had to lie to his face."

Jayne smiled "That doesn't surprise me about Jonas, but I am so glad you both understand, and I do believe it will be for the best, even though the thought of it is exciting."

"Indeed it will be, and the best from your point of view is yet to come." Janice grinned lasciviously.

"Tonight Jayne you will have a fly on the wall experience of my well hung darling husband, servicing his wife and our dear Mary, who has just this morning allowed me a glimpse into her secret playroom that she has kept a secret ever since Teddy first had it built several years ago now. And you my girl will have a front row seat through a set of two way mirrors; but for pity sake you had better keep quiet it is not soundproof and Tim will be blissfully unaware of you watching his performance, and fear not, we will position ourselves so that you have an uninterrupted view of the entire proceedings. Mary will no doubt show you the secret stairs that lead from the rear of her walk-in wardrobe to the back of the window room. However Mary and I want to be able to know that beyond the glass you will be as naked as we will be. So it's a no clothes night." Janice said wrapping her arms around her friend.

Jayne beamed in anticipation of being able to view the proposed evening's entertainment unheard and unseen by Janice's husband, a fantasy like so many she had discovered in the writings of her favourite author.

"Now concentrate and stop going all gooey eyed on me. Tim is coming at seven-thirty, and he is always punctual; so if you get the Grange by six we can all get warmed up, and I don't suppose you have used a sauna before?"

Jayne shook her head. "I've heard about them and often wondered what it would be like though."

"Well this evening Mary and I will show you; but just for ten minutes; it can get a little overwhelming if you

140

are not used to it. And now that's all arranged I must pop over and check with Mary about tonight's agenda. See you at six and don't be late we can have some fun together before Tim arrives."

Jayne glanced at the clock and saw that she had just over three hours before she was to be at the Grange.

The slow cooker with the beef stew for their evening meal had already been on for four hours and three more hours was enough time to get her and the dinner ready.

Rory had said he wouldn't be back until after six, so she would leave him a note and he could help himself.

She smiled sadly at having to choose eating with Rory, or watching her friend's being screwed every which way by the local doctor; who according to Janice had an enormous cock.

However the choice was easy dining with Rory was on the cards for another two weeks yet; but watching her friends being serviced was likely to be a one off event.

She also deduced that Janice's own fantasy was about to be fulfilled, and she wondered how, if Tim's cock was as large as it had been described; how would he manage to get it right up Janice's arsehole; but then Jayne calculated that it clearly wouldn't be the first time that Tim had fucked his wife's bum.

Only this time, Mary no doubt would have the big black strap-on dildo up Janice's fanny which meant her two holes were going to be stretched to the limit.

Jayne felt a cold trickle run down her inner thighs as the vision crept into her mind.

She quickly slipped her hand up her skirt and wiped it with her hand and began seductively licking her juice from her fingers,

She smiled as the wicked thought crossed her mind, of adding a little to the stew, and she pictured Rory unknowingly lapping it up.

"Jayne; you are a witch sometimes." She said to herself slipping her hand up her skirt again and looking round to ensure she was not being watched swished her wet sticky fingers in a glass of cold water before adding it to the stew.

As the appointed hour drew close, Jayne had a brief shower and slipped a thin cotton dress covering her nakedness.

Grabbing her heavy coat to keep out the chill, she hastened across to the Grange, where Janice and Mary were waiting impatiently.

Like teenagers having a sleep over, they hurriedly made their way up into the prepared sensually lit romper room.

Jayne was amazed at the sight that greeted her when Mary flung the door open. All the small windows had been blacked out, and the dividing walls that once separated the servants sleeping quarters had been removed leaving the whole lofty attic space as one large open room, and the mirrored wall at the far end made it seem even larger.

The complete floor area was carpeted in a deep lush pile cream carpet

The cabin-like wooden sauna stood to one side of the mirrors while a jacuzzi sat on the opposite side.

Three eight feet long white sofas were arranged around the room in an arc and a huge cinema screen covered the opposite wall adjacent to the door with the overhead viewer just visible in the high ceiling.

With huge Egyptian cotton towels round them they sat on the slatted wooden bench that ringed the super heated stoned sitting in its hearth, in the centre of the circular wooden cabin that was easily capable of accommodating seven more adults.

"Warm enough?" Mary said permitting her towel to drop behind her onto the slats; her larger softer breasts were already shining and dripping with perspiration.

"It certainly is." Jayne said sucking in the hot damp air and discarding her towel altogether before sitting with her feet up on the bench with her legs wide apart.

The sweat trickled down her body and soaked into the warm wooden slats before dripped silently onto the warm stone slab floor.

Janice lifted the small ladle of lightly perfumed water and poured over the heated lava rocks.

Jayne squealed as super heated air rushed up the centre of the small wooden room hitting the low ceiling before cascaded down over her head and body.

"Oh my god I can't breathe, its like being inside an oven." she gasped afraid that she might pass out.

"Its all right, it'll pass in a minute; but see how it allows the body to rid itself of the toxins and cleans every pore in your body. Just a few minutes more and we will cool off in the Jacuzzi." Mary said gripping the apprehensive Jayne's hand.

Jayne felt herself calm down as her body assimilated to the heat, and she watched fascinated as the stream of perspiration ran down Mary's chest and over her stomach before dribbling between her open labia lips and down through the seat slats.

"Mary it looks like you are having a pee." she giggled.

"Take a look at your own." Janice smirked leaning across and cupping her hand between Jayne's open legs, and seconds after lifting her hand full of Jayne's perspiration up for her to see.

"Enough now." Mary called sliding her bare buttocks off the wooden slats.

"Last one in the Jacuzzi is a wimp." She called rising to her feet.

Jayne being nearest the door was first out and she raced across the five yards to the waiting Jacuzzi and climbed the four steps and leapt into the unheated water.

She screamed as the coldness took her breath away and she quickly scrambled out, her nipples looking like organ stops.

"Its bloody freezing." she wailed catching the fresh towel Mary threw to her.

"It's supposed to be." Janice laughed "It closes your pores instantly."

Jayne's lips were blue as she watched both Janice and Mary undergo the same body jolting experience.

"Right then ladies let's have a settling drink and I think we need to complete our ablutions for tonight's event, and I suggest that we both use a little of the lubricant we bought the other day." Mary said with a shrewd smile.

With the warming towels wrapped around them they made their way down the stairs to the master bathroom and minutes later were giggling gratefully as the warm water washed their sexual orifices.

Refreshed inside and out they returned to the romper room, up the narrow hidden staircase set at the rear of Mary's walk in wardrobe and up into the small but equally comfortable room behind the mirrored wall.

Jayne quickly realised that the room had been constructed with one purpose in mind, and she wondered just how Teddy and Mary had planned to use it.

Over the years she had heard Jonas casually mention the parties Teddy had thrown for his old city friends. But as the years passed Teddy had become something of a recluse, wanting to spend all his time with Mary.

Jayne saw that the silent wall clock read seven fifteen.

"Time for the fun to begin, now Jayne for all our sakes please be quiet, and enjoy yourself." Mary said kissing her fully on the mouth before she and Janice slipped through the sliding mirror door and disappeared back into the Romper room; leaving Jane alone in the darkened room.

As the mirror door closed Mary pressed the tiny switch that turned the mirror from Jayne's side into clear glass.

Initially it was a little unnerving, seeing the huge wall turn into clear glass, until she saw that her friends on the other side were visually oblivious to her existence.

Confident that she was to all intents and purposes, completely invisible; Jayne took up her position on the well positioned easy chair.

At first she wondered why the bespoke chair had two longer armrests, until she deduced that that they were for her to put her legs up onto.

Placing her legs on the rests, she giggled comprehending that the sauna, combined with the two large whiskies she had consumed had left her a little tipsy and she felt wonderful.

Watching her friends who it appeared had forgotten of her existence, and she fleetingly felt a little left out, as they continued to sexually touch each other while they waited the few minutes for Tim to arrive.

Frustrated Jayne caste her eyes around the room lit only by the low lighting from the larger room through

145

the windows, and discovered a small low table beside her chair, that had a bottle of water and two of the sex toys they had purchased in Salisbury.

She recognised the smaller two pronged blue one was the silent vibrating rabbit, that would fit up her vagina and its attached companion would stimulate a couple of inches inside her bottom.

The other toy was flesh coloured and decidedly thicker and was a deeply ribbed replica of a larger than average penis.

She decided that perhaps she might not use the rabbit up her bum; she knew she wasn't as relaxed about it as Janice although she loved the feelings it created throughout her body.

The door bell resonated from downstairs made Jayne start, and Janice gave her a thumbs up sign as she disappeared down the main stairs to fetch her husband.

Leaving Mary sat on the edge of the Jacuzzi waiting impatiently with her fingers teasing between her open legs, for Janice to return with Tim into their den.

As the door opened Mary winked at Jayne through the mirrors and climbed down to greet him.

Jayne was already breathing heavily with anticipation and she leant forward to watch as her friend's expertly and sensually divested the grinning man of his clothes, which Janice carefully folded before placing them tidily on the end of the sofa.

Jayne pressed her hand to her mouth, and gasped as Tim's huge erection swung out from his knee length boxer shorts, it was enormous in length and girth its thickly veined shaft rose like a Greek column with a blue ringed shining dome that pulsated with every beat of his heart.

Mary unable to resist its beauty kissed its small mouth, at the top of the dome; the tip of her tongue dipping greedily into the oozing tiny open mouth.

Naked with his rock hard shiny knob well above his navel, Janice gripped his manhood he fingers unable to circumvent his shaft, led him into the heated sauna, and out of Jayne's sight.

The image of Tim's exceptional penis made Jayne wet and with her legs perched on the armrests her fingers slowly caressed her erotically aroused love button.

Smiling to herself as the image of Tim's enormous cock flitted through her erotic mind, she reached down to the small table and brought the larger ribbed penis shaped firm rubber cock and lifting her legs back up along the rests, and with her eyes closed she slowly inserted it into her wet open cunt, until it filled her love hole completely.

Still with her eyes closed she began to stroke it deeply into her body and drawing it back until just the tip of the domed head sat nestling inside her lips, before repeating the sensual insertion again

The ridges rippled over her engorged clit and up the inner walls of her vagina, sending wave after wake of pleasure deep inside her body.

She took a sudden deep intake of breath as she realised that in her imagination Tim's face had been replaced by Rory's as she thrust the ribbed toy faster and deeper inside herself.

Her passion bubbled over as ever more fantasies of herself and the beautiful man she fully accepted that she had fallen in love with, and she continued to make love with Rory in her own secret fantasy world.

"God that is so good." she mumbled as an orgasm cascaded through her arching body.

As the quivering inside her eased; she again became conscious that she should be quiet; and momentarily satisfied she slowly withdrew the penis from her wet vagina, and with Rory's satisfied face in her mind she began licking her own sweet juices from his imagined shaft.

The sound of the sauna door opening brought her eyes wide open and she held her breath as she witnessed Tim's long soft dangling cock as it plunged beneath the surface of the ice cold water.

Tim's long intake of breath and the look of shock that filled his face almost her want to laugh so to stop any involuntary noise she pushed the head of her toy into her mouth.

Janice and Mary eased themselves into the cold water for the second time, while Tim with a much-shortened penis clambered out and stood shivering with a towel round his shoulders

Mary climbed out next and after a quick rub down with a towel strode to where the still shivering doctor stood watching as Mary's gently bouncing breasts approached.

Mary sat back on her heels in front of him and pulled his soft shrunken penis into her mouth.

It responded like a clown's sausage balloon being blown up, as it swelled and stretched until it was hard and stiff again filling Mary's small mouth beyond its capacity.

Mary removed her mouth from the knob and pulling him down onto his knees she grabbed her ample breasts on the outsides and wrapped them around his prick clamped it firmly between them.

Dipping her head forward she took the blue ringed knob enthusiastically back into her mouth.

Her cheeks were drawn in as her tight mouth sucked hard on as she rode his cock between her soft breasts, continually sucking his hot knob until his long drawn moans of pleasure filled the room.

Jayne in hiding and aroused by the vision that confronted her, again pushed the realistic penis deep inside her expectant cunt.

The faint moan escaped her lips that thankfully went unheard by the trio outside.

With Mary sitting on her heels caressing Tim's cock between her soft breasts; Janice lay on the floor behind her, and wetting her forefinger, she circled Mary's anus brushing the tiny wrinkles that aroused Mary's hole to fractionally expand.

Tenderly Janice began pressing the tip of the forefinger into the epicentre, pushing then relaxing, then pushing a little harder each time, feeling it slowly relax until abruptly her fingers slipped easily inside Mary's receptive arsehole.

Mary gasped with pleasure and shuffled her legs further apart to allow Janice to began thrusting her finger deeper and deeper into Mary bum.

Tim's cock was beginning to jerk.

"Mary stop before I fill your mouth." Tim urged pulling his cock from Mary's mouth and breasts.

Mary drew a deep breath, and bore down pushing her bottom further towards the source of her enjoyment.

"Janice please don't stop." She begged lifting herself up from her couched position and bending over the edge of the Jacuzzi.

"Deeper and harder; please put two fingers up me now." Mary beseeched her own fingers rubbing her exposed clitoris vigorously.

Tim with his eyes fixed on his wife's fingers stretching Mary's anus with each stroke, eased Janice away from Mary's buttocks, and aimed the end of his large domed knob against the relaxed open arsehole.

Pushing himself forward until he felt Mary stiffen as her arsehole tightened against such a blunt intrusion. Tim relaxed and momentarily drew back relaxing the pressure, before again pressed forward his knob pressed hard against the small reluctant hole.

Janice squeezed an inch long piece of gel from the lubricant tube and massaged Mary anus and the tip of her husband's hot penis.

Resting her chest on the sides of the Jacuzzi Mary hands reached back and she pulled her buttock cheeks a far apart as she could.

Tim once more leant into her, and the sudden surge forward and the sharp intake of Mary breath revealed that Tim's massive prick was now fully embedded inside Mary's arse.

"Don't move for a minute." Mary gasped as she willed her anus muscles to relax and accept the insertion.

For several seconds they stood still as Mary flexed her anus muscles, allowing the pain of the intrusion to subside.

"Now Tim, but do it slowly." Tim felt the tightness of Mary's anal ring squeezing his shaft.

"Oh that's it do it again right up me. A little faster and push it all the way up." She gasped pushing her lower body away from the edge of the Jacuzzi and resting her head on her arms.

Tim gripped the sides of her waist and pulled her back onto him each time he thrust his pelvis slapping noisily against her quivering buttocks.

Janice seeing the gap between Mary and the Jacuzzi squeezed into it and sat with her legs apart and her mouth pressing against Mary visually throbbing exposed clitoris.

Juice from her anal fucked friend's cunt trickled freely down Mary's inner thighs.

"Tim do it as hard as you want, I'm coming." Mary screamed as Tim's rock hard cock pounded her arsehole, her breasts bouncing wildly and her legs spread wide apart as Janice continued to stretch her sensitive clitoris with her lips.

Mary suddenly gasped and sucked in volumes of life giving air as she bucked like a horse being broken, and her out of control body began its minute long continuous orgasm

Slowly withdrawing his still solid length of muscled flesh from the older woman's arsehole, the resounding plop echoed round the room as it flipped out. Now unsupported by Tim's penis, Mary's legs buckled.

From behind the mirror where the unobserved Jayne sat still pushing the dildo in and out of her own sloshing fanny, she could see Mary's angry red abused arsehole with its cave like dark interior pulsating.

With his arms wrapped around Mary's thighs Tim knelt down and caressed the raw looking hole with his tongue, as the still quivering Mary pushed her bottom back further.

Finally Mary gasped "Tim please enough I need recover, and that doctor has to be the best injection I have ever had." She whispered trying to get more air into her starving lungs and enjoying the soreness of her anus that brought far more pleasure than pain.

"Mary you have a delightful anus and believe me it was certainly as pleasurable for me as it was obviously for you."

The both helped pull Janice to her feet.

"My turn next." she said her own breathing coming in sobs.

"In a moment darling, we all need to recuperate, and having to explain a heart attack in these circumstances would not be easy." He laughed.

"Mary while we relax can I watch you suck Janice's cunt?" Tim asked.

Janice looked gratefully at him.

"Yes please." she whispered as she lay on her back with her feet almost touching the mirror, while Mary straddled her and with back of Janice's knees behind her elbows Mary pulled her friends legs up until Janice was almost doubled in half with her exposed fanny and stretched arsehole on full view, for Jayne to gaze at from behind the mirror.

While Mary dipped her head down between her friend's legs; Tim lay on his side his eyes just inches away from the noisy action.

Out of Jayne's sight Janice's own tongue circumvented the slowly closing hole of Mary's arse her tongue pushing its way inside.

Jayne climbed silently from the chair and knelt with her nose almost pressing against the glass watching intently with Tim's head less that twelve inches from her own, separated by a plate of fifteen millimetre glass, watching a Mary sucked and caressed Janice's almost white clitoris, pausing only when she felt Janice was about to orgasm, before taking her back again to the brink.

Janice herself barely managed to hold back her orgasm, wanting to save it for her personal finale.

Finally Mary and Janice fell apart and all three lay exhausted on the thick cream carpet.

After several minutes spent recovering from their excesses, Janice rolled on her side to face her husband.

"Now Tim I want exactly what you gave Mary, only I want you to come right up my bum, and Mary if you put that strap of cock on. No not that one, the biggest one. I want to feel it up me and stretching my cunt."

"Why in front of the mirror?" Tim asked "When we have all this room?"

"I want to be able to watch in the mirror as well." Janice said bending over Mary's who now lay on her back with her legs bent and the tip of the strapped on enormous black dildo resting against the opening to her fanny.

"No hang on I have a better idea." Janice said clambering up off the recumbent Mary.

"Let's use the massage table, and then Tim won't have to kneel." She said dragging the white leather table from behind the Jacuzzi and placing the end almost against the mirror, leaving just enough room for her husband to stand and pump his cock comfortably up her arsehole.

Mary scrambled on her back to the edge of the table her feet balanced on the corners, while Janice again knelt over her facing each other.

Tim positioned himself at the end of the table and smoothed a little of the gel over the end of his throbbing knob, while Mary wriggled into a comfortable position.

Jayne behind the glass sat with her head forward and found if she leant slightly to the left or the right she could see everything.

Her eyes fixed intently, as Janice's dark tanned arsehole stretched and relaxed as Tim pushed his knob worked it way slowly against the natural reluctance tight tiny hole.

Jayne was astounded at the thought of something so big could ever get into such a small tight orifice, and yet millimetre by millimetre she watched as Janice's anus stretched until suddenly she saw the blue rim of Tim's knob disappear inside her bum, which instantly clamped tightly round his shaft.

Janice gasped for a moment. "Now you Mary." She begged Mary pushed her pelvis forward.

"Oh yes push harder; that's it. oh my God that feels so good." Janice squirmed her cheek resting against her friends

Jayne watched intently as the thick black replica slid in and out of Janice's soft red cunt.

Jayne hardly daring to blink in case she missed something.

As Mary's upward strokes became faster, Tim's prick began its long slow slide deep inside his wife's arsehole until Jayne saw his balls slap against the narrow bridge between her cunt and arsehole.

Janice gagged as both of her holes were filled to capacity and Jayne saw her muscles bear down as she demanded ever more.

"Oh yes fuck me now." She urged them both. "Harder please more." she pleaded desperately the initial pain of her anus had been overwhelmed by the gratification he mind and body demanded.

Mary's upwards were strokes were slow but steady, while Tim's slow strokes became faster and faster until he was slamming his pelvis hard against her buttocks.

The sounds of their wet sex filled the room, as he continued to push his long thick hard prick deeper and deeper into Janice's demanding hole, while Janice

154

continued to scream like a demented banshee for more.

Suddenly a long drawn out shriek erupted from her dry mouth and she shuddered violently for what seemed forever before visibly sagging.

Tim stopped with his cock deeply embedded inside her until her orgasm waned.

"Don't stop yet Tim. She whispered "It's fucking beyond anything before and I want you to shoot your spunk up my arsehole."

Her words seemed to spur him on and he again returned to pounding himself in and out of her visibly reddened hole while perspiring Mary continued to slowly push her replicated penis up Janice's sopping wet hole.

Janice felt Tim's strokes quicken further, and she knew he had gone beyond the ability to stop, and she clenched her anus muscles gripping his cock tighter, and with several short jerks he yelled loudly as his balls emptied.

Jayne counted each of the ten spurts that drained him completely, and her own self induced orgasm was silent but fulfilling as she worked the rabbit in erotic unison on her fanny and her virginal anus.

Chapter 14

"My you look exhausted." Rory said looking up from his newspaper.

"Not training for a marathon are we?" he added noticing that Jayne was not wearing a brassiere and her thick coat had failed to keep the cold completely away from her breasts.

"Me run a marathon? You really must be joking, but we did a few exercises in the small gymnasium that Mary has at the Grange."

Jayne didn't quite see it as a lie; a manipulation of the truth possibly, but not a downright lie.

Then she recalled the fantasy she experienced earlier, and she hurriedly folded her arms across her chest.

"Your friend seems to have almost everything over there. I suppose there is a swimming pool hidden somewhere as well?" Rory smiled.

"Well yes there is, but it's drained for the moment, Mary only uses it during the summer months."

"Really, and here's me thinking that I had made a joke. Just goes to show how much I know what actually goes on in this little corner of old England."

"How was dinner?" Jayne asked wanting to change the subject.

"Superb, there's plenty left. Here let me warm it up for you, while you park your bottom by the fire you look frozen." He said getting up.

"Yes it is a bit chilly, and I just slipped into this old dress without thinking; Mary keeps the Grange at a constant temperature and it is never cold." Jayne replied stealing a warming sip from his half empty whisky glass

"Anything other than the usual misery in the newspaper?" She asked hoping her chest would soon be warm enough for her unfold her arms.

"I was just about to read an article about the bishop; it's at the bottom of the third page. I gather from the little I managed to read that he is planning a trip abroad, but that's as far as I got, before Cinderella arrived home from the ball." He laughed as he ladled out the stew into two bowls.

"Waste not, want not." He said placing Jayne's overloaded large bowl into the microwave oven. "And it really is a damn good stew." He added, watcher her reflection in the microwave door.

"You bastard." Jayne squealed crushing the newspaper in her hands.

Rory spun round, alarm spread over his face. "What! me" he exclaimed.

"No not you; oh I am so sorry Rory, of course its not you; it's that husband of mine. I see here that the bishop is taking his symposium to Australia and New Zealand, and according to the reporter; 'The Reverend Jonas Beech, will be accompanying him along with his widowed daughter Annabel Crouch' a frosty old crow who reminds me of Yvonne de Carlo, when she played Lily Munster; only a lot fatter and decidedly uglier." Jayne fumed.

"Jonas hasn't rung has he?" She asked trying to think rationally and curiously wondering just why Jonas hadn't bothered to telephone to tell her, before the press had been informed.

"Are you really annoyed with him?. I suppose you must be to be that vitriolic?" Rory said cautiously, still reeling a little at the thought she had been referring to him, and now knowing his secret was still safe, his heart rate slowed appreciably. And he offered up a silent prayer of thanks that she hadn't discovered the contents of his new novel.

A novel was so different from his sexual writings of the past, but still he had no intention of ever publishing it. Just writing his thoughts and dreams into words helped him deal with the fantasies that had been developing ever since Jayne opened the door on that first day.

"Angry with him; certainly, not with the fact that he is off to the Antipodes. No and to be honest with you; and I know this is probably the most unchristian thing I could ever say. But since he left I have felt so much better, no hint of the depression that used to haunt me at regular intervals. I have never laughed and felt so good about myself as much as I do now since I can't remember when. And yes a lot of those feelings are down to you, as well as my friends Janice and Mary along with others I will be making within the widows and Orphans group. No Rory life for me has changed beyond belief, and I was dreading the thought of returning to my old life. And I really am so very sorry for exploding like I did. But that guilty look that crossed your face when I swore; now that was funny."

Rory smiled sickly at the thought of Jayne reading the loving words he had written about her, once again filled his mind, and he turned sharply back to the

158

microwave feeling the memory of his words having an obvious visual effect on him.

"Yes I admit I was rather shocked." He said trying to adjust his steadily increasing erection into a less visible position.

His turn to the oven had been just a millisecond too late.

Jayne's eye had caught the flicker of movement inside his pair of grey chinos, and she smiled inwardly, and pulled the newspaper across her chest.

Then it struck her. Why had her playful suggestion that he looked guilty, should have triggered such a reaction, unless of course he had something to feel guilty about?

"What are you going to do about Jonas?" Rory asked wanting desperately to change the subject and take his mind away from the hidden novel.

"Nothing; I will wait until I hear from him. No doubt he will be in touch soon enough. But what will this mean for you. Will you be expected to remain her as temporary vicar or god forbid they send someone else." Jayne asked feeling her nipples had returned to their normal size.

"Come on your dinner is ready and I shall join you, and we can discuss my situation later." he said sidling to the kitchen table with the two steaming bowls held lower than one would expect.

He gratefully slid into his seat his embarrassment hidden by the table."

"Oh no more let me help you be seated?" Jayne giggled struggling out from the small armchair.

"Sorry my mind was elsewhere." He apologised.

"Obviously; but you are most certainly forgiven."
Jayne smiled knowingly, and she saw a slight flush
rising up his neck.

Neither spoke as they demolished the remainder of the
stew.

"Pudding?" Rory asked opening the oven door.
"Apple crumble." He said pulling the two individual
ramekins out.

"I shouldn't I am stuffed. But if you insist. Cream or
custard?" Jayne said attempting to get up from the
chair.

"Sit." Rory commanded. "I am the waiter, and I have
decided that it will take too long to make custard so it
whipped double cream."

"Oh Rory I do wonder how I existed before you came
into my world." Jayne said before realising the
significance of her words.

Rory face puckered in thought and decided that it was
time to change the subject; after all she was a married
woman.

"About my future." He said. "I have no idea what it
holds at this moment in time and as far as I am aware I
was only supposed to remain here for another ten
days, but perhaps someone will inform me before
then, and if I hear nothing then I shall stay here until I
am told different."

"If you leave then so shall I." Jayne suddenly blurted
out. "Heaven knows where I shall go but I am certain
that Mary would put me up until I can decide what I
want to do with the rest of my life. But I know now
that Jonas will certainly not be a part of it. I realised a
few minutes ago that I know now that I ever loved
him. Oh I convinced myself I felt something for him,
because he was someone safe, and after my life before

160

Jonas I needed someone safe. I must have known he was a bully. Not in the physical sense, but rather mentally domineering and unappreciative of almost everything I did. And I deduced that he had a number of what I believe were brief liaisons with other women, all older and rather larger women.

Rory's eyes raised in surprise but said nothing; he knew Jayne needed to express everything now she had committed herself.

"I remember years ago when I discovered a magazine dedicated to those types of women, under his study desk. But when I asked him about it; he said he had found it in the graveyard and intended to burn it. All those little things I consciously ignored and buried them beyond my memory."

Rory had stopped eating with his loaded spoon held halfway between his bowl and his mouth.

"Oh Rory I am so sorry I never meant to burden you with my problems, but reading that article was the final straw. So do you think I should move out of the vicarage tomorrow?"

Rory put the spoon back down into the bowl.

"Jayne I really think the first thing you should do would be to eat your crumble, and then I think we need to talk seriously afterwards"

His soft eyes fixed on her own made Jayne's love for him welled over her and she felt tears forming in her eyes, and she prayed silently that he couldn't read her mind."

They never spoke until both bowls were empty, and Rory placed them in the sink.

"Right young lady let's grab some more of the bastards whisky and decamp to the lounge, where there is a roaring fire just waiting to warm your outsides now that dinner had done us inside.

With a full-unopened bottle of Jonas's whisky, Rory led her into the lounge and sat her in the soft easy chair beside the fire.

With a glass almost full to the brim he placed it beside her and sat opposite in an identical chair.

"Right Jayne I know you are not under the influence of alcohol. Yet." He added his face more serious that Jayne had ever seen it previously.

"So I must assume that you statement at dinner was made in all seriousness."

Jayne nodded and sipped her whisky enjoying it all the more knowing that Jonas would be outraged to see her drinking what he deemed to be his whisky.

"So I have to ask if you have really thought it through, I mean taken everything into account."

Jayne shook her head.

"No I suppose not, but I do know that my marriage to that obnoxious prick is over. Sorry I didn't mean to swear I forget sometimes that you are a clergyman." she giggled as the whisky began to take effect.

"Fuck me being a clergyman." He swore back at her.

And she raised her eyes in horror followed by a cheeky grin, hearing Rory cuss made her whole body quiver, and she took a long draught fro her glass.

"Jayne believe me I am a man first, and a man who cares about you. So if you want to cuss and swear like a trooper, go right ahead, and if you run out of words I am sure I can bring a few more to the table."

"Rory you are so unlike any clergyman in the entire world and I love you all the more for it." Jayne stopped and stuttered "You know what I mean." She added lamely.

"Have another drink and let me finish explaining the dilemma you find yourself in." Rory replied his heart racing as he digested Jayne's impulsive words.

"Sorry." Jayne apologised her glass now almost empty.

"So you want to walk away from Jonas, well as you know clergymen are not paid an enormous stipend. Yes we get a free house and a number of other perks, but actual cash is limited. Therefore any settlement is likely to be minimal at best."

Jayne nodded sipping her refilled glass.

"Do you have any idea what Jonas has in the bank or in other assets?" He asked.

"I know his father left him a substantial sum several years ago and Jonas has always been careful with money, except when it comes to his car."

"You mean the old Aston Martin in the garage."

"Yes it was a car his father bought brand new in back in 1957 and it spent the next fifteen years sitting in the garage. He was much like Jonas, would never admit if he was wrong or had made a mistake. I did hear that he only ever drove it the once, and apparently its speed frightened him. Eventually he gave it to Jonas when he graduated, and Jonas loves that car more than anything else in the world. But I do recall many years ago when the insurance premiums went through the roof and there was something to do with the inland revenue, and his accountant suggested that if he put it in my name the premiums would be appreciably cheaper, I really don't know much about it but he did change the ownership to my name, and I have no idea if he ever changed it back, but I don't think so because the details always comes in my name, as did road tax to, but because its so old he doesn't have to tax it anymore, and as far as I can recall that's about everything. But I am not bothered about money; I have spent most of my life without much and I can always get a job."

"For the moment I would do nothing, just wait and see what Jonas has to say; but perhaps you should go through his private papers and see exactly what is what. If you like we can do that in the morning or would you rather make a start tonight." Rory asked.

"Let's take a look now." Jayne said excitedly her voice beginning to slur.

With glasses in hand they made their way through to the study.

Jonas's personal filing system was impeccable and they easily discovered his thick folder containing his bank statements, which revealed that in fact Jonas was certainly not a poor parish vicar, but he had a vibrant investment portfolio, and its last estimate amounted to almost three quarters of a million pounds.

"Fucking skinflint." Jayne slurred under her breath and Rory stifled the giggle. It still sounded strange hearing the beautiful vicar's wife cussing like a drunken squaddie.

"Here's the car document." He said pulling another folder from the cabinet.

"You were right it is in your name, so legally you own the Aston Martin."

There was little else of value or interest in the cabinet. Jayne tugged the deep bottom drawer.

"Jonas always keeps this locked, but I saw him put the key on top of the bookcase once." She said trying not to slur her words.

Rory stood up and swept his fingers along the bookcase, and smiled as the small key touched his fingers.

"Let's see what secrets your bastard Jonas has been keeping from the world." He said turning the key in the lock and pulling the draw fully open.

"Oh dear." he said attempting to close it before Jayne could see what was inside.

Jayne quickly jammed her foot in the drawer."

"Do you really want to see them?" Rory asked grinning blatantly.

"Too bloody right I do..." She said lasciviously looking at the large pile of sexually explicit magazines, all of older larger women in every possible pose revealing all their delights for the camera."

"I don't think 'you' ought to look at them." Jayne howled with laughter. "They might corrupt you."

"Actually I was corrupted years ago by just such a lady, Celeste de Abbeville was her name and she was a real lady who actually used to pose for just these sort of underground magazines, and truthfully I have always believed that the female form in any guise is a truly wonderful thing. But I am only telling you this because Jayne you are as drunk as a skunk and you won't remember it in the morning."

"I wouldn't bet on it." Jayne giggled.

Rory lifted the pile of magazines from the deep draw.

"There's a box underneath." he said picking out an A4 photographic paper box.

"What have we here; more secrets no doubt?" He said lifting out the top one of the two black plastic envelopes that were inside.

He saw at first glance that there were approximately thirty full colour photographs.

"Just more of the same, only it looks like these were done privately." He murmured flicking through them.

Jayne snatched them from his hands and held them up to his face.

"Recognise any of the faces?" she asked her face shocked beyond belief.

"No not really should I?" he asked trying desperately to place the assorted faces.

"Yes that one looks like the lady who always sits in the second row at Sunday service. Who is she? He asked, recalling the round full virtuous face smiling at him as he delivered his sermon.

That's Beryl Bainbridge the wife of the local butcher." Jayne grinned.

"So that's probably why she has that ring of black pudding halfway up…"

"Rory; I asked if you recognise the face not the rude bits." Jayne giggled and decided that she had better not drink anything else but a strong coffee.

"Let's take these to the kitchen, I think I need to sober up a little, and anyway I am frantic to pee." Jayne giggled and laughed even more, when her legs refused to cooperate.

Rory desperately wanted to laugh, but restrained himself. Instead he lifted her to her feet and her legs wobbled.

"Here let me get you up the stairs to the toilet." He said making his way to the stairs.

"Please be quick I am bursting." Jayne giggled again.

Rory swept her up into his arms and carried her up the stairs the edge of her unrestrained breast held innocently by the tips of his fingers.

Opening the door with his elbow he sat her onto the toilet.

"Don't forget to take your knickers down." He said as she struggled to lift her dress away from the toilet seat.

"Got none on." She giggled inanely again.

Rory could contain himself no longer and he began laughing until tears streamed down his face."

The sound of water splashing noisily into the pan only brought on further bouts of laughter.

"What's so funny about a woman with no knickers on talking a piss?" Jayne said shaking her head in an attempt to clear the blurry vision.

"Nothing at all, but Jayne its no wonder I love you so much."

Jayne stopped in mid stream."

"What did you say?" she asked her mind trying to digest what she imagined she heard.

"Nothing; just finish what you are doing and I'll make you some strong black coffee."

"But you said…"

"That you are a lovely woman. Now can you do the rest yourself?" Rory asked wishing she would say no.

"Of course I can; I know I have drunk far too much, but I can still wipe my own fanny? See." she said grabbing the roll of toilet paper and pushing her hand between her legs.

Rory lifted her of the seat and again carried her back downstairs into the kitchen.

An hour later and after an unrecalled number of mugs of strong black coffee, Jayne made it up to the toilet one more, this time under her own steam.

"You sound a little more like your own self." Rory said as she returned to the kitchen and considerably happier that she was at least able to converse in an understandable manner.

"Ok now that we are lucid again let's see who else you recognise. This one should be easy." Jayne said covering the image of the large breasts with three inch light brown areolas and much darker brown nipples that the woman held up for the camera in her thick fingered hands.

"That's the lady at the post office, she's the one that talks as if butter wouldn't melt in her mouth. "Rory gasped, your husband certainly managed to get the most unlikely women to pose for him.

Jayne went through the first envelope naming each woman by name.

"That's Judith Charlesworth, her husbands a retired general, whose suffering from advanced Alzheimer's. Jayne said, and stared in total disbelief at the next photograph.

"Oh dear me, well this is one lady I would never have guessed would take part in this set up, but you never really know about people do you?"

"Who is she?" Rory asked wondering if the large woman had ever trimmed her bush anytime during her life.

"That dear boy is none other than professor Anastasia Whitley-Smyth PhD M.D and several other more letters as well, and she is the head of psychiatry at Salisbury University. She is also the owner of Dellside Cottage on the far side of the village. She is also probably the only one you will never see in church. She claims to worship the devil and the dark side of life. There were rumours a few years ago that she ran a witches coven in Blackdown wood, but no one ever caught them in there.

Turning to the next photograph Jayne smiled

"This extremely attractive voluptuous blonde woman is Agnes Downes, a farm workers wife and mother of eight children, the youngest is now ten years old. And this one you must know is Akela otherwise known as Ethel Hunt a short barrel of a woman who according to Jonas's photographs is a keen fan of anal sex."

Rory looked vacant his eyes taking in the object she had protruding from her bottom looked like a wooden rolling pin.

"Cubs? Brownies?" Jayne asked again covering everything on the photograph except the face.

"Of course she's the lady that runs the cubs and brownie packs."

"For an intelligent man you can be a little slow at times." Jayne chuckled.

The remaining photographs were a collection of the same women if different sexual poses.

They sorted through them all and placed the photographs in their separate piles and found there were approximately five explicit photographs of each of the six local women.

"Well that's one lot of very liberated ladies taken care of." Rory smiled.

"You are not in the least bit embarrassed are you?" Jayne said, lifting the second of the black plastic envelopes from the box.

"Should I be? I think they are all very desirable in their own way." He grinned

Rory took the shiny package from Jayne's hand and slid them out onto the table.

"Jesus Christ!" he gasped trying to retrieve them.

Jayne was too quick for him snatched them from the table.

Her face almost convulsed as she flipped quickly through them.

"Of course I can guess who that one is with the post mistress's breast in his mouth, his photograph is on his study wall, along with this one" she said disbelievingly.

Pulling another photograph from the pile, Rory reached across and took it from her hand.

"This one is obviously the witch lady who is happily peeing into his mouth of who must be your dear husband, and the one whose rather small member she is chewing on is indeed none other than the bishop. You have to admit they take rather a nice photograph, but one has to wonder who actually took the photographs."

Probably the pub landlord's daughter Rosie, that's the large girl in this next photograph mind you she's hardly a girl, must be in her mid to late forties by now. Never married and by the look of her in these other shots never needed to." Jayne laughed.

But it has to be her, she is a rather good with a camera, and has several of her wild life photographs published in a number of magazines." Jayne said smiling at the photograph of the bishop bent over the general's wife knee while she posed with a riding crop in her hand, and judging by the red weals across his scrawny rump, she had beaten his backside extremely hard.

"Rory I know I shouldn't laugh, or pass judgement. I mean we all have our secrets and I certainly wouldn't want someone to laugh over mine. So let's put these back where we found them, and perhaps now we are sober enough we can relax and have another drink, but maybe just the one."

"Filled to the brim?" he asked.

"Of course." Jayne laughed.

They packed up Jonas's photographs attempting not to laugh at some of the facial expressions, and once everything was back in its place, Rory put the key into his pocket.

It was the chill in the room that woke Rory and a chink of light from the closed curtains illuminated the sleeping Jayne sprawled out in the chair opposite.

Her bottom had, during the night slid towards the edge of the seat lifting her dress up almost to the top of her thighs.

Rory ran his tongue around the inside of his mouth in an attempt to remove the fur that coated it.

He rubbed his knuckles hard into his eyes to clear them.

As the blurred effect cleared he saw that the small shaft of light from the gap in the curtain behind him shone directly between Jayne's spread legs.

He had forgotten that she had admitted to not wearing any knickers. And unable to resist he lay back gazing lecherously between legs, his eyes focused on her partially open labia lips with the wisps of dark hair framing them.

He felt his body instantly react, and he deliberately closed his eyes and stood up.

Stepping across the front of the cold dead fire he reached up and attempted to ease her dress down back over her knees.

Jayne stirred and opened her eyes and seeing Rory's just inches from her own she lifted her head and kissed him full on the mouth.

"That's for last night, and for being a perfect gentleman." She said.

"It wasn't easy being a gentleman, and Jayne for reasons that are personal to me, I want to be as honest with you as I can."

"Why have you been dishonest?" Jayne said sitting up and frowning while pulling her dress down to reinstate her modesty.

"Yes I have been deceitful with my feelings towards you. I have tried desperately to avoid my emotions taking control of my common sense; and like you yesterday; in the early hours of this morning I too came to a decision about my life. I lay unable to sleep last night I as I sat watching you sleep and I rehearsed a speech over and over again; and it was a speech I never thought I could have the courage to make."

Jayne's eyes misted over guessing that he was about to tell her he was leaving.

"Well I suppose I should get the hardest part of my decision over with first, then maybe the rest won't mean anything."

"And?" Jayne asked feeling her tears beginning to course down her pale cheeks."

Rory took a deep breath and put his hands on her trembling shoulders.

He swallowed hard and in a quiet almost whispered voice said.

"Jayne I have to admit that from the moment you opened the door just a few weeks ago, I have been totally in love with you. I tried desperately not to be, but the more I tried the harder it became"

Jayne couldn't hold back the flood any longer and she began to sob uncontrollably."

Rory fingers dug unconsciously but cruelly into her shoulders.

"I am so sorry Jayne, but I had to tell you how I felt before I left, otherwise it would have haunted me for the rest of my life if I hadn't told you how I felt."

He tried to release his hands from her shoulders but she grabbed his wrists and held them tightly until her sobbing had subsided.

And she lifted her tear stained face to his and she looked into his sad haunted eyes.

"Rory I too felt the same way, and for weeks I told myself that it was an infatuation that would evaporate, but it didn't, it just kept getting harder and harder to deny it to myself."

He lowered his face and the sadness from his eyes was gone, replaced by one of hope and love.

Jayne threw her arms around his neck and Rory's arms encased her upper body.

They kissed slowly and with a passion that went far beyond anything sexual.

"Jayne I want you to be my wife, my lover, my friend, and even my mother sometimes. I want you to be my everything.

"Yes, oh yes." She spluttered and began sobbing again.

Rory picked her up in his arms and carried up to his bedroom.

Chapter 15

It was late afternoon when Rory finally opened his eyes to discover that he was alone.

"He looked round wildly wondering if it had all been a dream, and then he sighed with relief as his eyes lighted on Jayne's folded dress on the chair.

His nostril caught the aroma of bacon cooking drifting up from the kitchen below."

As he opened the bedroom door. Jayne called up. "Ready to eat yet sleepy head?"

"I'm as hungry as a butcher at a vegetarian banquet."

"I can't see why, you almost devoured me last night." Jayne called back up to him.

"That was hours ago, and a growing man needs continual sustenance."

"Well I've heard it called many things before, but that is a new one on me."

Dressed in just his jeans Rory bounced down the stairs.

"There's a letter for you." he said picking up the single envelope from behind the door.

"Does it have a return address?" Jayne asked.

"It most certainly does, and it's from Jonas."

Rory just managed to catch the breakfast plate before it crashed to the floor.

"What does it say?" Jayne asked wiping her hands on the kitchen towel.

"I have no idea it's addressed to you. Do you want me to open it?"

"Please." She said wringing her hands together.

"Stop worrying there is absolutely nothing he can do to us." Rory said, "And if you want I will talk to him. There is no way he can intimidate me."

"Oh thank you, I don't think I am strong enough to speak to him. I have spent too many years just doing whatever he wanted me to do." Jayne admitted nervously.

Rory slit the envelope open with a breakfast knife and extracted the single sheet of handwritten paper.

He briefly scanned it.

"Well the first thing is we are in luck, because Jonas also wants a divorce, and he puts it plain and simple. A straightforward divorce, but the catch is he wants you to admit fault, and he wants it as quickly as possible. He is willing to offer you. Now get this, five thousand pounds in cash if you will agree to it."

"The fucking bastard." Jayne hissed.

"Young lady your language is becoming positively human." Rory laughed. "And he wants you to arrange for the garage to collect his car to be shipped to Perth in Australia, apparently he has been offered a post out there, and get this, he wanted to be the first to tell you that once the divorce is final he intends to be married to Annabel the bishops daughter. He also writes that he will be by the telephone at seven-thirty this evening for you to ring him, and he has written the number down." Rory placed the letter on the table and wrapped his arms around Jayne's quivering body.

Jayne's face reddened with fury.

"Now before you blow a gasket let me explain what your terms will be." Rory said turning off the gas under the burning bacon.

"But if you, ring him now he will know that something has been going on between us."

"Of course he will, and I am guessing that was his plan all along. I thought it strange that I was chosen to replace him, when there were far more qualified curates just waiting for such an opportunity, and didn't I overhear your friend Janice saying something about the doctor keeping an eye on you, and this symposium. I assume that was an excuse to leave us alone together. They obviously did their homework on us both, which makes them far more astute that they would have us believe. So on second thoughts I won't telephone him, in fact we will let him stew for a few days, while I sort out a few things.

From the hotel desk three days later an extremely irate Jonas retrieved the letter addressed to him personally in Jayne's unmistakable ornate handwriting.

Retreating to the empty hotel lounge to where he could read it in private, he smiled to himself knowing that Jayne would have done everything he demanded of her.

He tore open the envelope, his face went from fiery red to deathly pale in a split second as he gagged and recognised the several postcard size copies of his photographs that fell onto the floor.

With rasping breath and a severe pain across his chest he scrabbled around on his hands and knees until he recovered them all and quickly shoved them in his pocket.

He slumped into the chair and slowly unfolded the letter in the event that more photographs might be inside.

Finally safe in the knowledge that all the snapshots were in his pocket he nervously read the letter.

Jonas,

I will keep this letter as brief and as much to the point as I can.

When I read your letter I was pleased to read that you wanted a divorce.

Which is certainly something I am not averse to. However your terms are in no way acceptable.

So I shall list my own and suffice to say more copies of you the bishop as well as your lady friends, who I must admit did surprise me, but not quite as much as your bishop friend, are already in envelopes with accompanying letters.

Thanks to the local newspaper, I have the address of your new parish in Perth, and of course the Archbishop of Canterbury's address is well known.

So going through your personal papers and which I thought was incredibly stupid of you to leave them behind, but no doubt in your haste to be with your desirable Annabelle, who surprisingly was not amongst your collection of photographs.

But then cavorting on film with the bishop's penis in the landlord's daughters mouth, while you feasted between her legs is perhaps not the brightest thing you have ever done.

However enough of the compliments.

According to your bank statements and other documents you have close to three quarters of a million pounds in an investment portfolio

So let's say for the sake of clarity that should you have to sell.

You would raise somewhere in the range of half a million pounds and you will agree that I am being extremely generous with my calculations.

And under the laws of the land as you wife I am entitled to half of that amount.

Now we come to the question of my car.

Yes the one sitting in the garage it's the only car I legally own, if you recall several years ago you put its ownership in my name.

Apparently it is a rare and much sought after vehicle, as I discovered when I rang a vintage car auctions after I received your letter.

Two hundred thousand pounds was a conservative estimate.

In fact the Auction house offered me that much, unseen.

Now as I see it. If you pay me half of what you have stashed away, of which I am prepared to accept two hundred and fifty thousand pounds.

And if you really feel you can't do without my car; I am willing to part with it for the same amount the auctioneer offered, which brings it to a total of four hundred and fifty thousand pounds.

You have until tomorrow night, which is the tenth of the month to agree fully with me terms. I will not in ay way shape or form accept a penny less.

You will then have another seven days to have the money deposited into my account.

Failure to comply fully with my generous offer will result in the letters being posted at six pm on the tomorrow evening, and my car will be sent for auction as soon as possible afterwards.

You need not call or contact me the only contact I want is to see my bank account receive the four hundred and fifty thousands pounds. Then I shall send you all the copies of your collection to you. However any delay in the money being in my account will result in the letters being posted.

Jayne.

Chapter 16

Luck plays an important roll in life, and for the bishop it was lucky that it was he who discovered the collapsed body of his friend with the letter clutched in his hand rather than any of the hotel employees or other guests.

The shocked Bishop managed to understand the single word that Jonas managed to utter before slipping into unconsciousness

The bishop hastily scanned the letter and rifled through the dead Jonas's pockets and retrieved all the photographs.

Later in his room after he had consoled his daughter Annabelle he burned them along with the letter in the toilet.

The telephone call he made to Jayne that same evening was brief telling her curtly that Jonas had suffered a terrible stroke and had passed away soon after reaching hospital and the point of her letter to expose him was now unnecessary.

He did however have the audacity to ask what she intended to do with the copies photographs still in her possession.

Jayne ignored the question and put the telephone down on him.

The Aston Martin fetched three hundred and twenty five thousand pounds, and Jonas's lucrative portfolio continues to generate a fairly healthy income.

The new vicar who took over St Matthias's church was a youthful forty year old thin man, with a chubby but pleasant wife, and their five young daughters.
It was his first ceremony at the church to marry Rory and Jayne.
Rory gave up being a clergyman, the hours were too long was his excuse.
The day of the wedding the church was full to capacity and summer blooms filled every crevice.
With Tim as his best man and Janice and Mary as matrons of honour, who giggled like schoolgirls who admitted to Jayne that they had come without wearing any knickers.
Jayne whispered over her shoulder that she hadn't any on either.
Mary opened the banqueting room at the Grange for the wedding festivities, and Jayne was quick to notice the eight unsmiling and anxious faces of Jonas's models with the exception of the Professor who had refused her invitation but had graciously acknowledged the copies of the photographs and the short note that explained that the negatives had also been destroyed.
During the afternoon Jayne managed to entice them separately to one side, and quietly explained that she had burned a box of Jonas's photographs and a whole set of negatives.
With embarrassed smiles of gratitude they thanked her, and they brightened up appreciably more when Jayne suggested that they might find it intensely

pleasurable to join the widows and orphans group; it being a far safer way to enjoy the fruits of life, without the fear of embarrassing exposure and emphasising her suggestion with an obvious knowing wink.

At different times during the evening's festivities she saw them individually in enthralled conversations with either Mary of Janice.

The Rik Kolling revelations between them turned out to be something of a damp squid.

Each other guessing that they had been found out. just a week or so after Rory's admission to be a writer, and Jayne's ownership of one of his novels. The book Religious Desires she left under Mary's pillow before they left for a new life in Thailand.

Where not for the money as thanks to Jonas's timely demise they had an income that sustained them in great comfort, but they wrote just for the hell of it, and they resurrected Rik Kolling from the place where Rory had abandoned him years earlier.

Rik's return from the dead was welcomed in certain literary circles not only in the Far East but also in some of the small villages that abound in England, and elsewhere.

When Jayne attempted to tell Rory about her dual sexuality, he had smiled knowingly and told her that he had known almost from the outset.

"The three of you were as obvious as a lake in a desert, and I loved you all the more just knowing how you loved one another." He had said whilst they made love.

Jayne and Rory pride themselves on the fact that their pasts have all been revealed to each other, even Rory's darkest days which initially were painful but had the effect of cleansing his soul was how he put it.
Now they use their experiences to allow Mr. Kolling to bring fun back to those bored with mundane lives.

Both Janice and Mary keep Jayne up with the state of the Widows and Orphans group which is finding enthusiastic members from the most unlikely places, and their descriptions of events is a constant source of material for Mr. Kolling.

Tim is still unaware that his dalliance with Mary and his wife, was witnessed not only by the vicars wife, but also by numerous well placed hidden digital video cameras, and he knows nothing of the fact that Mary and Janice often relive that memorable evening on the huge cinema screen in the romper room.

Janice happened to overhear Eric in the Crowne bar relating his innuendoes to his usual group of bar flies, and after a brief word with him in the car park later, he readily agreed to stick to posting letters and cleaning windows.
No one ever knew why Eric no longer voiced his innuendoes, but a whole section of the village breathed a sigh of relief.

Jayne's regret that she believed she could be past child bearing age has been shattered, as at forty two she is expecting twins, but neither she nor Rory want to know what sex they are until they are born